The Ultimate Desktop Publishing Starter Kit

Anne Fischer Lent

Addison-Wesley Publishing Company

Reading, Massachusetts • Menlo Park, California • New York
Don Mills, Ontario • Wokingham, England • Amsterdam
Bonn • Sydney • Singapore • Tokyo • Madrid • San Juan
Paris • Seoul • Milan • Mexico City • Taipei

Library of Congress Cataloging-in-Publication Data

Lent, Anne Fischer.
    The ultimate desktop publishing starter kit / Anne Fischer Lent.
        p.   cm.
    Includes index.
    ISBN 0-201-41032-X (paperback)
    1. PagePlus.   2. Desktop publishing.   I. Title.
    Z253.532.P34L46   1995   95-891
    686.2'2544536--dc20   CIP

Sponsoring Editor: Kathleen Tibbetts
Project Manager: Sarah Weaver
Production Assistant: Erin Sweeney
Cover Design: Barbara T. Atkinson
Text Design: Peter Blaiwas
Set in 10.5 point Stone Serif by Greg Johnson, Art Directions

1 2 3 4 5 6 7 8 9 -MA- 9998979695
First printing, May 1995

Addison-Wesley books are available for bulk purchases by corporations, institutions, and other organizations. For more information please contact the Corporate, Government, and Special Sales Department at (800) 238-9682.

This book is dedicated to Greg, Steven, and Jeffrey.

Acknowledgments

Desktop publishing, by its nature, is best when done through the collaboration of several people. That way, each person can offer his or her input on the design, writing, printing, or other element according to his or her expertise or interests. Creating this book was no different. Without the help and support of several people, *The Ultimate Desktop Publishing Starter Kit* would never have gotten off the ground.

First of all, several of the technical aspects of this book would be incomplete without the input of my good friend and technical consultant Stan Miastkowski of the Peterborough Technology Group. The wolf logo used in the Fischer Lent Communications examples was created by Roger Goode of the Proper Pup Studio. The software included in this book is the brainchild of Gwyn Jones, Serif's president and founder. Several of the PagePlus-specific tips came from PagePlus wizard Scott Prive, also of Serif. And finally, the book itself was pulled together with the help of Claudette Moore of the Moore Literary Agency and was completed through the diligence of Kathleen Tibbetts at Addison-Wesley.

A great big thanks goes to my three guys, Greg, Steven, and Jeffrey. Jeffrey Robert was born between chapters 2 and 3, and proved to be just the kind of baby every writing mom needs. And yet another thanks to my mom, Loraine, for pitching in whenever the going got tough.

Anne Fischer Lent

Contents

Introduction

Desktop publishing is the relatively new art of assembling text and graphics on a personal computer. Up until the 1980s, page assembly was done by traditional typesetting methods—text was output in single columns, and the columns were waxed and stuck to the page. Production artists would manually position the type around illustrations and create page breaks.

With the advent of the microcomputer, or the personal computer, came the lay person's ability to output type in different fonts and sizes. As microcomputers progressed technologically, they became more adept at creating graphics. Soon page-layout programs became common, not only for publishing books and magazines, but for creating newsletters, brochures, and more.

Now desktop publishing is ubiquitous, and it seems everyone is getting into the act. Anyone with a computer capable of running a word processing or desktop publishing program can now produce desktop designs, regardless of whether they know anything about design or page production. In this book you'll be introduced to some of the elements of good design, which you can apply to the various sample projects offered in the following chapters.

Until recently, desktop publishing was done primarily on the Apple Macintosh because of its superior graphics capabilities. But the IBM PC has caught up in its graphics sophistication, and today desktop publishing software programs are equally numerous for IBM PCs and Macs alike. *The Ultimate Desktop Publishing Starter Kit* focuses on creating desktop publishing projects using an IBM PC or clone, rather than a Macintosh.

About the Software

Accompanying this book is a copy of PagePlus 3.0 from Serif, Inc. PagePlus 3.0 has three levels of use—Introductory, Publisher, and Professional. The designs in this book begin with the Introductory level and move up through Professional. The enclosed copy of

PagePlus includes all three levels; however, it can only be used for a limited time. Once you install the software you can use it for 60 days; after this point you'll have to call Serif to unlock your own registered copy (see Appendix D for more about upgrading).

During the 60 days that you can use the enclosed software, you will have all the functions of PagePlus 3.0 at your fingertips. PagePlus 3.0 won a Seybold Award for Excellence at the 1994 Seybold Seminar on Desktop Publishing, where it was noted for its technological advancements and real-world applications. In addition, PagePlus 3.0 has been acclaimed in the computer press as having all the elements you need for basic desktop publishing in a low-cost package. PagePlus 3.0 costs hundreds of dollars less than the high-level desktop publishing packages with which it competes successfully, which is why we chose it as the best software to include with *The Ultimate Desktop Publishing Starter Kit*. This book, however, was written and published independently of Serif and PagePlus, and is not meant to be an endorsement of the product. See Appendix E for information on how to choose among the leading desktop publishing software packages.

About This Book

This book is written for anyone who has a need to produce desktop designs on a PC, whether for corporate, small business, or community use. I've attempted to serve two needs here. One is to provide a resource and reference book on the basics of desktop publishing that can be used by anyone, regardless of computing expertise or choice of software. I've tried to use terminology that is understandable to anyone, and where that was difficult, I've attempted to define the technical jargon. At the back of the book is a glossary and acronym dictionary, which should help clarify some of the technical talk a bit more.

Second, *The Ultimate Desktop Publishing Starter Kit* will serve as a primer for creating useful desktop-published materials using the accompanying PagePlus software. The book's hands-on approach invites you to work along at your own pace. And rather than using words to describe what you should be seeing on your PC screen as you create a project, I've included a multitude of screen shots to show you just what steps to take. In addition, hints and tips provide shortcuts or advice that will help you make the most of your desktop projects. Hints and tips are sprinkled throughout the book. Hints are bits of advice on how to do something better, such as choose the best type of paper for a specific design. Tips apply to making better use of PagePlus.

Computer design skills are not necessary. In fact, the book is written for the person who has very little understanding of the way a computer works. Chapter 1 explains what you'll need in terms of computer equipment, printers, monitors, and such. While many people who are new to desktop publishing already have computers and printers, it's important to know the demands desktop publishing places on your equipment to determine whether it needs a face-lift or replacement.

Chapter 2 tells you everything you need to know to get PagePlus up and running. It also includes some tips on making the most of your computer's memory.

To help you get started actually publishing, Chapter 3 guides you through the elements of page layout, text, and type, and how to use photographs, illustrations, and other art for graphic impact. Once you have the basics of design under your belt, you're presented with the basic tools and functions of desktop publishing, in Chapter 4.

With your hardware set up, the software installed, and a basic understanding of the elements of page design, you are ready to embark on a hands-on training session you can follow at your own pace. Ten chapters, each devoted to a different project, teach you how to design a postcard, a ticket, stationery, forms, a poster, a press release, a greeting card, a brochure, an advertisement, and a multi-page newsletter. All of these lessons can be adapted to meet your individual needs. The final chapters help you go beyond the basics, with information on four-color design, special effects, tables, drawing applications, and more.

The world of desktop publishing on the PC is all here for you. I've charted the course, but you can set the pace. Go from start to finish, if you'd like. Or jump from the preliminary chapters to the lessons that pertain specifically to the design you wish to create.

Each lesson assumes you've learned a bit from the previous one, but the step-by-step screen shots will provide you with several handy reference points if you want to jump around. No longer will your output look like everyone else's. With a little desktop publishing finesse, you can add a personal or professional touch to all your documents. Good luck and happy creating.

The Ultimate Desktop Publishing Setup

The first five chapters of *The Ultimate Desktop Publishing Starter Kit* are intended to help you set up the ultimate desktop publishing office and get some basic desktop publishing knowledge under your belt. This section of the book can stand alone as a desktop publishing primer and should be kept close at hand for quick access to the many facts and pointers you'll want to reference as you get going.

Starting with the system, you are offered practical advice on how much equipment to get and what you probably don't need. Adding peripherals can be a daunting experience for those who are new to technical products. In Chapter 1, each piece of the desktop publishing puzzle is described, so you can go out shopping armed with the knowledge you need in order to make intelligent buying decisions. Before you can use the software included with this book, you need to have a CD-ROM drive and know how to use it. Chapter 2 outlines just that. Chapter 3 concentrates on design, while Chapters 4 and 5 get you grounded in the basics of PagePlus.

Chapter 1

Before You Start

The fully equipped desktop publishing office is a far cry from the bare-bones setup you can get away with for word processing and other basic office chores. Before you get started, you should examine what you have, determine what demands desktop publishing will put on your existing equipment, and decide what you need to upgrade or replace.

This chapter examines each component in the desktop publishing office, from the system to the drives, monitor, mouse, keyboard, scanner, printer—and even the paper you use for printing. For each component, we'll examine what your needs might be and what the range of choices is. For example, if you plan to produce four-color multipage documents with lots of graphical elements such as photos, tables, and charts, then you'll need a system with some graphics power. If you'll be spending a lot of time looking at your designs on-screen, then you'll want a system with a top-quality monitor. Of course, you'll want to make sure you have optimal input and output equipment. Printers run the gamut from low-cost dot matrix printers to high-end laser printers. To properly equip your desktop publishing office, knowing how you'll use each component is as critical as knowing how each one works. This chapter will focus on each piece of the desktop publishing puzzle. At the back of the book, you'll find a resource guide that lists some of the manufacturers of the equipment mentioned in this chapter.

The System of Choice

A basic rule of thumb in setting up a PC-based desktop publishing office is to select a system that will run Microsoft Windows well. Windows is a graphical user interface that runs on top of DOS (the operating system). To make the best use of Windows you need a system with a fair amount of power, because Windows lets you "multitask," or run several applications at the same time, in different windows. Running Windows on barely adequate hardware will cause great pauses in your work and can cause additional problems besides; for example, you might get GPFs (General Protection Faults), which are error messages that tell you Windows has crashed. Usually they only affect the application you're currently running, but they often cause you to lose your work. Many desktop publishing and graphics programs run under Windows, so let's take a look at what sort of system you need to run Windows effectively. For each piece of your desktop system, I'll suggest a bare-minimum configuration, as well as the optimum.

Let's begin with the CPU, or central processing unit. This is the core of your computer system, its engine. PCs and PC clones are for the most part based on the 8000 family of processing chips. The chip determines the computer's speed, which is measured in megahertz (MHz). The slowest you can purchase is 25 MHz or 33 MHz, which is sufficient for Windows. Today you'll commonly find systems with a 80486-based CPU (also called just 486 or the Pentium chip). Years ago the 80286 was state-of-the-art, but not only can you no longer purchase a new 286 machine, it's difficult to use one with Windows. Sure, you can run Windows 3.1 on a 286, but you'll spend a great deal of time contemplating the Windows hourglass, which tells you to wait while Windows finishes some internal chore.

Before seeking the right hardware for Windows, think about why you want to run the graphical user interface in the first place. It may be to take advantage of its multitasking capabilities (running more than one application at the same time), to get enhanced graphics (higher resolution and more colors), or to run one or more of the many applications written specifically for Windows. First of all, while Windows will run on 80286-based systems, you won't be able to multitask. To take advantage of multitasking, you need to run Windows in enhanced mode, which requires at least an 80386SX system.

The Bare Minimum

If you already have anything higher than an 80286-based PC, you may be able to make minor modifications to it to meet the minimum system requirements for running Windows. Your system should be at least a 25-MHz 386SX with 4 MB of RAM (random-access memory), a 100-MB hard drive, a 3½-inch floppy drive, a 14-inch VGA monitor, and a mouse. Each part of your computer can be upgraded; for instance, you can upgrade the RAM by adding more memory, you can get a higher-capacity hard drive, and you can install a larger and higher-resolution monitor. But be aware that while upgrading your old system to a Windows-capable system is possible, it is best done by a skilled computer professional.

If you do need to buy a new Windows-ready system, you're actually in luck, because you can get more for your money now than you could a few years ago. When you set out to buy a new system, a good rule of thumb is to purchase the most system you can afford. Your minimum standard should be a 66-MHz 486 with 4 MB RAM, a 200-MB hard drive, a 3½-inch floppy drive, a 14-inch Super VGA monitor, a video accelerator card, and a mouse. Keep in mind that this configuration is only a minimum.

The Optimum

The most recent version of Windows is Windows for Workgroups 3.11. This version has several advantages over previous versions of Windows, but it is fast becoming the Windows standard based on its speed alone. According to Microsoft, the minimum configuration for Windows for Workgroups 3.11 is a 386 with 640K of RAM, 1024K of extended memory, 8 MB of free hard-disk space, and at least one floppy disk drive. Microsoft does not recommend this configuration if you're going to add other components or be on a network, which would render this minimal configuration below minimum standards for most uses. It's also important to be aware of the minimum configurations for applications. Word for Windows 6.0, for example, requires at least 4 MB of RAM and 25 MB of hard-disk space for a full installation. Imagine running four or five of these standard applications side by side, and you get the picture of what you really need in your system.

The optimum configuration for a desktop publishing system is at least a 60-MHz Pentium system with at least 8 MB of RAM, a 500-MB hard drive, and a mouse. If you'll be doing a lot of desktop publishing and can afford it, going with 16 MB of RAM will make a big difference in performance. Computer prices have fallen so low today that a system equipped with what sounds like an incredible amount of power can be purchased for under $2,000. That price, incidentally, often includes a Pentium CPU, a CD-ROM drive, a sound card, speakers, DOS 6.2, and Windows for Workgroups 3.11.

Memory

Unlike DOS, which only uses the first 640K of RAM, Windows uses all the memory you have. So, the more RAM you have the better. PC memory (or RAM) is usually made up of SIMMs (single in-line memory modules), which are plug-in modules with memory on them. You can think of RAM as your computer's short-term memory; for example, when you're working on a desktop publishing project, whatever is active on your screen, such as fonts, graphic elements, or text, before it has been saved to the hard drive, is resident or is being run in RAM. You need at least 4 MB to run Windows; but, as mentioned previously, 8 MB is better, and 16 MB is better still. The more powerful the system, such as a Pentium system, the more RAM you want in order to take advantage of that power. When you run Windows in enhanced mode, the processor uses either the RAM or the hard disk as "swap space" for the applications and other processes it has to handle simultaneously. It's much faster to use RAM for swap space than a hard drive, so the more RAM you have, the better your system's performance.

Upgrading memory is possible, as I mentioned previously, but it isn't always simple. Memory is added by plugging SIMMs into the motherboard, and most systems can be expanded up to 64 MB. Some even come with an extra slot for an add-on memory board, so you can add almost as much RAM as you want (or can afford).

Hard Disk Drives

Computer systems usually come with two drives: a hard disk drive and a floppy disk drive. The floppy disk drive, usually for 3½-inch disks, is the toasterlike mechanism you feed floppy disks into. They are necessary for installing software or rebooting the system in an emergency. But you'll mostly rely on the system's hard disk drive for storing your desktop publishing creations. Before purchasing a system, make sure that the hard disk drive that's offered with it is adequate for your needs—now and in the future. The capacity or storage space on the hard drive is measured in megabytes; today's common choices range from 270 MB to 540 MB. Again, a good rule of thumb is to get the largest hard drive you can afford. The more desktop publishing work you do, the more storage space you'll need.

If you are going to upgrade an existing system with a bigger and better hard drive, you have a choice of SCSI (small computer system interface) or IDE (integrated drive electronics). IDE drives are easier to install, but SCSI drives outperform them. SCSI drives are also known to be more flexible, because you can connect up to six other SCSI devices. SCSI drives cost more, however. The IDE format is more common for lower-capacity hard drives (200 MB and lower). Installing a hard disk drive is best left up to a skilled professional.

CD-ROM Drive Basics

CD-ROM (compact disc–read-only memory) drives seem to be the latest craze, and for good reason. Based on optical technology, CDs let you store up to 660 MB of data. CD-ROM drives use prerecorded discs that are very much like music discs, except that they store digital text and graphical data. Write-once drives are now on the market, which let you write to the CD, but these new drives are very expensive.

New systems often come with CD-ROM drives already installed, and a lot of software today is available only on CD. Before purchasing a CD-ROM drive, think carefully about your uses for the technology. If you're planning to buy a new system that comes with a CD-ROM drive preinstalled, you're in luck. You don't have to give the CD-ROM drive much thought, because it is already integrated with the rest of the system. You won't have to worry about installation and setup hassles. On the other hand, if you have an existing system and you want to add a CD-ROM drive to it, you have several decisions to make.

First of all, determine your uses for the CD-ROM drive. There's a lot of hype about multimedia systems, but use caution. Unless you plan to play 3-D games, run video clips, and keep multitudes of CD-based encyclopedias at your fingertips, you probably don't need to set up a full-fledged multimedia studio complete with stereo sound. You should, however, make sure that any CD-ROM drive you purchase has certain characteristics. The list below can be used as a guide to purchasing a new CD-ROM drive.

How to Choose the Right CD-ROM Drive

INTERNAL OR EXTERNAL

When you look for a CD-ROM drive to add to your existing system, you have a choice of an internal or external drive, as well as a choice of speeds. Internal drives are handy, because they don't take up additional desk space. However, you must have a spare drive bay in your PC in order to install one. If you purchase an external drive, make sure it comes with a cable that is long enough to reach from your PC to wherever you want to place the drive.

SCSI

You may want to stick with a SCSI (pronounced "scuzzy") drive rather than going with a nonstandard drive. SCSI drives are usually faster, and they are not limited to a single manufacturer's technology.

SPEED

The lowest-cost drives are single-speed drives, but they have been made obsolete by the popular double-speed drive. Recently on the market are quadruple speed drives; but again, for most desktop publishing applications you don't need to concern yourself with the latest (and most expensive) technology available. A double-speed drive will meet most desktop publishing needs.

Speed measurements that you should concern yourself with, however, are access time and data transfer rate. Access time refers to how quickly you can open and close the software on a disc; it is measured in milliseconds. Look for a CD drive with a low access time (195 milliseconds is sufficient). The data transfer rate refers to how quickly you can search through data on a CD, once you have opened it; it is measured in kilobytes per second. Look for a high data transfer rate (300 is usually sufficient).

XA

Look for a CD-ROM drive with extended architecture (XA) capabilities, which indicates not only that it is capable of playing multimedia CDs with sound and graphics, but more importantly, that it can handle more than just text.

Installing the CD-ROM Drive

Installing a CD-ROM drive, whether it's internal or external, requires working with DIP switches or jumpers and possibly installing a sound card. Then you have to make everything work with your software, which requires adding a device driver to your CONFIG.SYS file as well as a DOS extension called MSCDEX.EXE. As with other hardware peripherals, if you're not familiar with the workings under the hood of your PC, get a skilled computer professional to install your CD-ROM drive for you.

Monitors

With your system up and running, you should next concern yourself with installing the best monitor for desktop publishing. Your monitor is what you stare at as you do your work, so it is important that you get the best monitor for your needs. For desktop publishing, you need to display both text and graphics clearly and in realistic color, so that what you see on-screen is really what you will get in print.

If you already have a computer system, you probably already have a monitor. But you may want to take a critical look at it and determine whether it will meet your needs for desktop publishing. Most monitors that come with PCs are not adequate for serious desktop publishing. Many have only a 12-inch viewing area and have excessive flicker and glare, which causes a lot of eyestrain after long work sessions. If you plan to only occasionally produce desktop-published documents and can live with the small size, then you may be able to skip this section and stick with the monitor you already have. On the other hand, if you plan to do a lot of desktop publishing or other text- and graphics-intensive work at your computer, you may want to look into upgrading the monitor on your system.

Color is the only way to go these days. In fact, it's very difficult to find a monochrome (black and white) monitor that is capable of handling graphics. Monitor sizes you should consider for desktop publishing work range from 15 to 21 inches. Fifteen-inch monitors offer about 92 square inches of viewing area, or about 38 square inches less than a 17-inch display. This doesn't mean, however, that you see more on a larger monitor. What happens is that the image itself is bigger on a larger monitor. Thus the drawback to using a smaller monitor is that text and graphics are smaller.

Monitors vary greatly in overall quality and sharpness, as well as in price, so choose carefully. For example, good-quality 15-inch monitors today sell for about $400, 17-inch monitors cost about $800, and 21-inch monitors cost closer to $2,000 or more. With this range in prices, you'll want to arm yourself with information on what you need, before you start to shop. The following is a list of features and specifications to look for when selecting a monitor.

How to Choose the Right Monitor

ANTI-GLARE SCREEN

Many monitor manufacturers put a non-glare coating on the screen to cut down on the amount of glare caused by extraneous light. Some monitors also have an anti-static coating, which will cut down on the amount of dust the screen collects.

BANDWIDTH

The bandwidth is the measurement (in MHz) of the signal that is transmitted to the monitor. The higher the bandwidth, the lower the distortion of the image. Look for a monitor with a bandwidth of at least 100 MHz.

COLOR AND RESOLUTION

Color monitors are by far the most popular today. In fact, it's nearly impossible to purchase a new monitor with anything less than VGA color, which is composed of 640 x 480 pixels (or picture elements—the dots that make up the picture). A common resolution today is Super VGA, or SVGA, which is up to 1024 x 768 pixels.

DOT PITCH

On color monitors the dot pitch is the distance between the centers of the three colors (red, green, and blue) that make up the color display. Smaller distances indicate greater resolution.

EMISSIONS

The Swedish government has developed a set of guidelines called MPR II or Swedac, for maximum allowable emissions by monitors of VLF (very low frequency) and ELF (extremely low frequency) magnetic and electric fields. MPR II specs have become a standard, indicating that a monitor produces comparatively low levels of potentially harmful emissions. While the medical community has not officially agreed that emissions from monitors are hazardous to your health, many people feel it's better to be safe than possibly sick. Today, many monitors sold throughout the world meet the MPR II specification. If you're concerned at all about possible risks from monitor emissions, it's wise to look for a monitor that is MPR II compliant.

ENERGY EFFICIENCY

The Environmental Protection Agency (EPA) awards the Energy Star label to products that are manufactured with energy savings in mind. For a monitor to receive this label it must use 30 watts or less in standby mode. Standby mode is when the monitor is not currently being used, and its power usage automatically drops down from a typical 100 watts.

HORIZONTAL SCAN FREQUENCY

Measured in kHz, this is the number of lines displayed on a monitor in a one-second period. Monitors with higher resolutions should also have a higher horizontal scan frequency. Look for a monitor with a horizontal scan frequency of at least 30 to 65 kHz.

NONINTERLACED FORMAT

Look for a monitor that offers a noninterlaced format, which means that as an image changes on the screen, the monitor redraws each line of the image consecutively, as opposed to redrawing every other line, as in an interlaced format. A noninterlaced display has less flicker than an interlaced display, thus resulting in less eyestrain.

REFRESH RATE

The refresh rate, measured in Hz, is the same as the vertical scan frequency. It is a very important specification to look for when purchasing a new monitor. It indicates the number of times per second that the screen image is redrawn. Look for a monitor with at least a 70 Hz refresh rate—the lower the number, the more flicker and fatigue. The Video Electronics Standards Association (VESA) recommends 70 Hz as the minimum refresh rate for monitors with a resolution of 1024 x 768 pixels.

SIZE

Monitor sizes refer to the horizontal measurement of the entire monitor, rather than just the screen area, so you may want to actually measure the screen of a monitor before you purchase it to determine the actual viewing area. Many 17-inch monitors, for example, have an actual viewing area of 15½ or 16 inches.

Another possible size concern is the amount of space a monitor occupies on your desk. Monitors larger than 15 inches weigh about 50 pounds or more, so you won't be placing them on top of your computer. If the amount of space in your work area is a consideration, you may want to stick with a 15-inch monitor for this reason alone. However, if your desktop publishing work will include multipage documents, you may want to choose a monitor that is large enough to display two pages side by side.

VIDEO GRAPHICS ADAPTER

You'll need to install a video graphics adapter or video card inside your system to drive your monitor. A video card intercepts the data from your computer and converts it into the graphics signals that create the image on your monitor. Make sure the monitor's resolution and refresh rate match that of the card. Any card and monitor you install should also be capable of displaying 256 colors. In addition, most video cards come with special software drivers that you need to install when you install the video card.

Input Devices: Mice, Keyboards, and Scanners

Everything you see on the screen has to be input into the computer somehow. Input methods can be as rudimentary as typing at the good old keyboard, as simple as clicking a mouse, or as sophisticated as capturing color images on a scanner. Choosing the best equipment for each is often a matter of personal choice. The mouse and keyboard should be designed to fit your hands and should have a feel that you're comfortable with from the start. And when it comes time to look for a scanner, you'll want to understand the wide range of features available. Scanner technology has come a long way in recent years, and it's best to know what you need and want so you can take advantage of the latest innovations.

The Mouse

With the advent of graphical user interfaces (GUIs), such as Windows, computer screens are now typically loaded with little icons that you can click on by using a mouse. The more graphical (as opposed to textual) a software program is, the more you'll find yourself using a mouse instead of the keyboard.

A mouse is a little mechanical controller that you move across a surface, preferably a "mouse pad." As it moves, an electric signal is sent to the computer telling it the position of the mouse, or the mouse's "coordinates." When you move the mouse, you will see the corresponding mouse "pointer" move across the screen. To input a command into the computer, you move the mouse pointer to an icon and click on it, using one of the buttons on the mouse.

Using a mouse takes getting used to for many people. It means adjusting your thinking to controlling what's happening on the screen with what is rolling under your palm. Some people never seem to make the adjustment; fortunately for them, most software can operate both by keyboard and by mouse. For most people, however, the mouse is—or becomes—second nature, and they find that they can manipulate software much more quickly by a simple click of the mouse button.

Other Mice

A mouse is yet another device cluttering up your desktop. If you find that the mouse's cord gets in your way, you may want to opt for an optical mouse. The optical mouse is a cordless device that works in the same way as the regular mouse, but it is linked by an infrared beam to a receiver in your computer.

Trackballs are growing in popularity, as people search for input methods that are a better fit ergonomically. Trackballs work the same way as a mouse, but instead of moving what looks like a bar of soap around on a pad, you cradle a fixed ball beneath your palm. Rolling the ball around in its socket moves the cursor on the screen. As with the traditional mouse, trackballs also have buttons to click and include a cordless variety as an option.

The Keyboard

In most cases a keyboard comes with your computer system. You may not like it however, for several reasons. The "click" of the keys can be loud and annoying. The function keys (F1 through F12 or F15) may be at the top, when you're used to them on the side. Or you may be left-handed and want a keyboard with a layout designed more for the way you work. With all the different types of keyboards on the market, there is something for everyone. Let's take a look at some of the specifics.

The overall feel of the keyboard, including the sound the keys make, should be right for you. Sometimes keyboards take some getting used to—but they shouldn't be irritating to the point that they interfere with your work. Test out a keyboard before you buy. Make sure the keys strike right for you—are they too stiff or too loose feeling? How is the size of the keyboard and the keys? If you have very small or very large hands, you may want to look for a keyboard that is better suited to your size. Finally, how's the angle of the keyboard? Repetitive stress disorder is a common complaint of people who do a lot of typing at keyboards that are not perfectly suited to them. You can reduce the amount of strain your hands endure by getting a keyboard that "fits."

Key placement may also be a consideration for you. Function keys should be placed where you're used to finding them, so you don't have to search for them every time. The numeric keypad is important if you input a lot of numbers. Make sure it's located within an easy distance to the alphabetic keys, so you don't have to stretch to reach the numbers. One keyboard manufacturer has gone as far as to "break" a keyboard down the middle, so you can place the right- and left-hand sides at optimal typing positions.

QWERTY or Dvorak?

If you have not been trained on a traditional QWERTY keyboard (on which the layout of the keys in the upper left corner spell "Qwerty"), you may want to consider an alternative. The Dvorak keyboard places the most-used consonants and all the vowels in one row, so that most of your typing is done from that row. It was designed to speed up typing, because your fingers don't have to move as far to hit the most commonly used letters. Touch typists trained on QWER-TY keyboards would have to relearn this new method, however.

Left-Handed Keyboards

If you're left-handed, you may notice that function keys, numeric keypads, and other special keys are not placed with you in mind. Customizable keyboards are available that let you place special keys where you can get at them most easily.

The Scanner

While you can desktop-publish documents to your heart's content without a scanner, there will be times you wish for a way of "pulling in" a photo, chart, or other graphic so that it becomes an electronic image rather than a paper one. With a scanner you can take a photograph, scan it, and then place it within a document. Imagine the difference in a newsletter story on the employee of the month with a color photo next to the story.

As with other devices for your computer, scanners come in several varieties. The most common are the flatbed and hand-held scanners. The flatbed scanner lets you scan a document up to 11 by 17 inches by placing it face down on a glass plate, like making a photocopy. The scanner reflects light off the document back into the scanner, where it reads what's on the page one line at a time. Flatbed scanners scan at a rate of 300, 600, or 1200 dots per inch (DPI).

A hand-held scanner fits in the palm of your hand and lets you capture small sections of text or art. To capture a full page, you have to run the scanner down the page at least twice, in perfect side-by-side swipes. The advantages to hand-helds are their price (usually just a few hundred dollars) and portability. For serious desktop publishing work, however, their downsides can spell disaster. Hand-held scanners don't give you a precise scan of anything but a tiny image. For a bit more money, it often pays to equip your desktop publishing studio with a device that will output satisfactory graphics for your documents.

How to Choose the Right Scanner

The following is a list of what to look for in a flatbed scanner.

BUNDLED SOFTWARE

Scanners need OCR software in order to read text. You also may want image-editing and color-calibration software. Make sure that your scanner comes with what you need to get the job done.

RESOLUTION

Look for a scanner with a resolution of at least 300 DPI.

MONOCHROME, GRAY SCALE, OR COLOR

Scanners come in monochrome, gray scale, or color. Monochrome is plain black and white, while gray scale gives you varying shades of gray. If your desktop publishing work is, and will always be, in black and white, then a monochrome or gray scale scanner may meet your needs. But if you ever plan to produce color documents, go for a color scanner. Color scanners will also let you scan black and white line art and gray scale images. Prices of good-quality color scanners have fallen below $1,000.

PASSES

Color scanners vary in the number of times the scan head must pass over the document. A color scanner that calls itself a "single-pass" scanner will likely scan a color document more quickly than one that takes three passes to scan the document.

SIZE

If you need to scan legal-size documents, look for a scanner with this capability.

TWAIN STANDARD

Select a scanner that is compliant with the TWAIN standard. This standard lets all windows applications share a scanner. The standard ensures that the scanner works with optical character recognition (OCR) software, which is the software that recognizes type characters (and should do so regardless of font or type size). Desktop publishing, image editing, and other software that is TWAIN-compliant has its own TWAIN utility that works with your scanner. TWAIN utilities also allow you to make some adjustments to the image with brightness, contrast, and hue controls.

INSTALLATION, QUALITY, WARRANTIES, AND MORE

Other things to look for include ease of installation, quality of scanned images, length of warranty, and technical support. If you purchase a SCSI scanner, the SCSI board should be easy to install and the software should be up and running with a simple install program. To determine the quality of the scanned image, ask to see a sample. You should see very little difference between the original and the scanned image. Warranties vary, but are usually for one to two years. Technical support can consist of toll-free phone calls or on-site service. If a scanner is critical to your business, you may want to check on how many hours per day the support is available and what the average turnaround time is on repairs. You may be able to purchase a service contract that is tailored to your needs. For more information on scanners and other input devices, see Chapter 16.

Output Devices

You can create the most elegant designs imaginable, but without the right printing device, you can't do them justice. Some desktop publishers will take their work to a professional print shop for final output. These people may want to own a printer that is of sufficient quality to give them sample output, but not the finished product. Or they may want to output "camera-ready" copy themselves, in which case the quality of the output is fairly critical. Other desktop publishers will want to do it all on their desktop, which means outputting final copy right from the printer attached to the computer. This is only cost-effective and time-efficient, however, when you are printing relatively few documents.

There are only three basic types of printers to chose from. So it should be a simple purchase, right? Well, yes and no. Printer technology is fairly straightforward, and the leading manufacturers make high-quality, reliable products. But you should first understand a little bit about how each type of printer works and what its advantages and disadvantages are to know which type will meet your needs.

Dot Matrix Printers

The first advantage to dot matrix printers is the price. You can purchase a brand-name dot matrix printer for less than $300, while ink-jets start at about $300 and lasers at $500 and up.

Dot matrix printers work the most like the old-fashioned typewriter, using the same impact technology to create the characters, with an inked ribbon between the print head and paper and a platen bar that clamps the paper in place. Dot matrix printers use continuous-feed paper, which is both an advantage and a disadvantage. The advantage is if you need to print invoices, shipping labels, or other multipart forms. The disadvantage is that this type of paper is more likely to jam than the single sheets used in ink-jet and laser printers.

Another big advantage of dot matrix printers, for some people, is speed. Very fast dot matrix printers print about nine pages per minute, compared to about four pages per minute for some laser printers. To get that speed, however, you have to print in draft mode, which is not very high-quality type. In fact, some people find it unacceptable for printing business documents, let alone for professional quality desktop publishing. A 24-pin dot matrix printer will produce a higher-quality output than a 9-pin, although you may still not find the quality acceptable for printing preliminary drafts. You won't want to use a dot matrix for your routine destop publishing output, however.

A final, but very important, consideration in selecting a printer for desktop publishing is whether it is a PostScript printer. PostScript is a standard print language that lets you scale a variety of fonts and produce high-quality text. For PostScript ability in a reasonably priced and reasonably fast printer, you'll have to look only at laser printers.

Ink-jet Printers

Ink-jet printers fall in the middle between dot matrix and laser printers in terms of price, quality, and speed. They work by means of a print head that shoots a jet of ink onto the page. Good-quality ink-jet printers have a print head that pauses to let the paper dry before moving on. Many high-quality ink-jet printers print about 1½ pages per minute in draft mode, which produces considerably better output than draft mode on a dot matrix printer. Some ink-jet printers feature a drop-in ink cartridge, which makes changing the ink supply very simple and clean. The downside of these cartridges is their cost and the frequency with which you'll have to change them if you use the printer a lot. On the other hand, one of the biggest advantages to ink-jet printers for some people is how quietly they operate, especially compared to dot matrix printers, and also to some laser printers.

Laser Printers

Laser printers are the most sophisticated of the three types of printers. A laser printer operates very much like a photocopy machine. When you send a document to a laser printer, the computer stores an image of the document. The image is then sent to the printer, where a laser beam etches the image, one dot at a time, across the printer's drum. The drum holds an electrical charge, to which toner (a kind of powdered ink) is attracted. Paper moves over the drum and is printed with the toner. In many laser printers the drum and toner cartridges can be replaced simply and less expensively than an ink-jet cartridge. As mentioned previously, the need for PostScript compatibility makes this type of printer the only choice for producing camera-ready copy or directly producing final output. A second consideration is the print quality different laser printers offer. Some laser printers feature only 300 DPI (dots per inch) resolution, but many offer resolutions of 300 or 600 DPI, which you select on the printer or in the software.

How to Choose the Right Printer

COLOR

If you need to output your desktop publishing creations in color, you can choose from all three categories of printer. Desktop publishing studios that demand color outputs, however, will probably only be satisfied with the speed and quality of a 600 DPI color laser printer. Even with laser printers, however, you won't get a perfect match between the color you see on the screen and the color that is printed. Ink-jet printers can produce good color output, although some don't print the same colors that you see on screen. In addition, color ink-jets can be dreadfully slow. And, finally, the quality of a color dot matrix printer can be surprisingly good, but more smearing of colors occurs with this level of printer. You must scrutinize your needs and determine what price you're willing to pay in terms of speed, color quality, and, of course, dollars.

DRIVER

In most cases, when you install a new printer you must also install a new printer driver (which is software). Make sure that you have a driver that will work with your printer, or that one comes with the printer you buy.

EMULATION

Computers and printers communicate with each other using a page description language, or PDL. PostScript is one PDL, but there are many others. Choose a printer with a variety of PDLs so that you are not limited.

MEMORY

Many laser printers come with memory installed. One MB is the minimum you'll need for producing graphics, but 4 MB or more will allow you unfettered design possibilities. The memory in a printer is used for storing fonts. And the more you use the printer's fonts, rather than those stored in your computer, the faster your printing will be.

PAPER

Printers use either cut-sheet paper or continuous-feed paper. If you need to print large sheets of paper (11" by 17" is a common size), make sure the printer you choose will accommodate this size. In addition, check the capacity of the paper tray. Some trays hold only one hundred sheets at a time, while others can hold much larger quantities. Larger or additional paper trays are often options on many printers.

PRICE

List prices of printers range as widely as the print quality they offer. The lowest priced printers from the leading manufacturers start at list prices of around $300, while the highest priced laser printers that give you professional-quality output can cost as much as $10,000.

POSTSCRIPT

PostScript is a graphical page-description language developed by Adobe Systems, Inc. It uses mathematical relationships to produce scalable fonts and graphics that can be output in any resolution and on any type of PostScript-supported device. PostScript files tend to be much larger and take up more memory than standard files, so if you plan to output a lot of PostScript files, look for a printer with more than 1 MB of RAM and possibly as much as 4 MB.

PROCESSOR

Many laser printers come with either a 68000 or a RISC processor. The 68000 processors cost less, but RISC processors are faster. Depending upon how complex your graphics are and how you'll be using the output from the printer, you can decide if the extra cost is worth the investment.

QUALITY

Printer quality is measured in dots per inch (DPI). Printers with lower DPI measurements are lower quality; you can actually see the little dots that make up each character. DPI measurements generally range from 300 to 1200 DPI. Be warned, however, that all 300 DPI printers do not produce the same quality output. The dots produced by a dot matrix printer are larger and are placed less precisely than those from an ink-jet or laser printer. Ink-jet printers, while they produce better-quality output than dot matrix printers, produce characters that are more fuzzy edged than those produced by laser printers. The best way to judge the print quality is to examine several samples showing a selection of fonts.

SPEED

Printer speed is measured in pages per minute (PPM), from 1 PPM or less up to about 17 PPM. Another measurement of speed is characters per second (CPS), which ranges from 90 CPS up to about 720 CPS.

Is It Worth the Paper It's Printed On?

After you've carefully crafted your desktop creation, don't jeopardize its impact by printing it on less-than-optimal paper. Just as the wrong paper can detract from your design and lessen the impact of your message, the right paper can give your document a professional look. Paper companies have caught on to the desktop publishing revolution and are now producing what they label "desktop publishing" paper. These products tend to be overpriced, and fortunately there are several alternatives. Knowing what you'll be using the paper for is vital to choosing the right paper for the job.

For the Do-It-Yourselfer

If you'll only be printing samples from your desktop printer and taking the job to a service bureau or printer for final output, then you can run standard copier paper through your printer. If you are using your laser printer to create a document for distribution, you can use a paper that is specifically designed for laser printers. Laser printer paper is generally heavier stock and has a sleeker surface that lets the toner adhere better. One advantage to printing your final documents directly on your laser printer is that you can add a color to your desktop design just by choosing a colored laser paper.

The size of the paper you need is also an important consideration. Most laser printers handle paper in letter or legal sizes, and some let you feed smaller sizes manually. Most printers, however, do not let you load paper that is wider than 8½ inches, so if you plan to use 11" x 17", be sure your printer will accommodate that size.

In addition to running plain or colored copier paper or laser paper through your laser printer, you may want to look at paper that is preprinted with a design, such as the paper sold for desktop publishing. This paper is more expensive, but will give your document a professional touch.

Printing in Color

As mentioned in the section on printers, the color you get from a printer often varies from the color you see on-screen. This is because your printer uses cyan, yellow, and magenta to create printed colors. Your monitor, on the other hand, uses red, green, and blue to create the colors you see on-screen. On-screen colors tend to be brighter and more vivid, while printed colors are often deeper and darker. Using a high-quality paper designed for laser printing will give you the best results. Laser paper, as mentioned previously, is specially coated so the toner will adhere to it. Colors benefit from this coating as well, giving you brighter colors that are closer to what you see on-screen.

Going Outside

Most laser printers output at 300 DPI, while some produce 600 or even 1200 DPI. Printing a large number of documents on a laser printer is not cost-effective, however. Not only do you use large amounts of toner, which can be expensive, but you will place wear and tear on the print mechanisms, thus shortening the life of your printer. In addition, printing a large number of documents on a laser printer can be a long and tedious process. If your paper tray holds only 100 sheets of paper, you'll have to stand by to refill it ten times if you're printing 1,000 sheets. When your output demands better quality or you need to print hundreds of pages, it's time to take your work to a professional printer.

Types of Paper

Professional printers will have samples of papers they have in stock, as well as samples of specialty papers that they can order. You'll have a choice of many types and colors. The following are common choices:

NEWSPRINT

Newsprint is a low-cost paper that's most often used for printing newspapers. While inexpensive, this paper discolors easily.

TEXT

Text paper is best suited for printing black type alone, rather than colors and in halftones. Text is available in many colors and finishes.

COATED

While coated paper is very expensive, it will give you outstanding color. Coated paper comes in different finishes, from dull to glossy.

COVER STOCK

This heavy paper is made in colors and finishes to match text paper. It's used for book covers and anything else that needs to be on a thick stock, such as posters or folders.

BOND

Like the high-quality bond paper used in typewriters, this paper is available in many colors and finishes. It comes in sulfite, which contains wood fibers, or rag, which contains cotton fibers. Rag paper is the more expensive of the two.

Software Installation

The software that comes with this book is on a compact disc (CD). To use it, you'll need a compact disc drive. See the section on CD-ROM drives in Chapter 1 for information on how to choose the best drive for your needs.

To install the software that comes with this book, follow these steps:

1. Turn on your CD-ROM drive if it doesn't automatically turn on when you turn on your computer.

2. Insert the CD into your CD-ROM drive. How you do this varies from one CD-ROM drive to the next. Consult the documentation that came with your CD-ROM drive for specific instructions.

3. Start Windows.

4. From Program Manager, pull down the File menu and click on Run.

5. In the dialog box that pops up, type `D:\Install.exe` (substitute the correct drive letter for your CD-ROM drive if it's something other than D). See Figure 2.1.

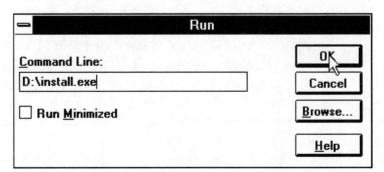

FIGURE 2.1 The PagePlus installation command line

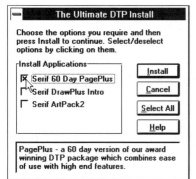 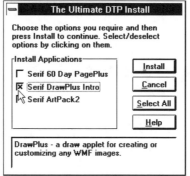 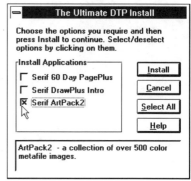

FIGURE 2.2 The PagePlus Install box

6. When the Install box pops up, choose to install the 60-day version of PagePlus, DrawPlus Intro, and/or the ArtPack. See Figure 2.2.

7. The CD will be installed in a subdirectory called `Serif` on your `C:` drive, unless you specify differently.

 **PagePlus TIP**
When you install PagePlus 3.0, you also get a copy of PagePlus Intro, which you can use for an unlimited time.

8. Choose which options you want to install, and press Install (Figure 2.3). Note the amount of free disk space needed for each item. Also note that the Install program tells you how much free disk space you have available on your system. To follow the tutorials in this book, you'll need to install all the files for now. You can uninstall those you don't need later.

What's on the CD?

On the CD is a time-limited, unlockable CD version of PagePlus 3.0. This is a full, working version of PagePlus 3.0. It comes with 25 fonts, templates, and more. You may install it once and use it for 60 days, after which time you may call Serif to unlock the unlimited version of PagePlus 3.0. See the information listed in the registration window in PagePlus or call 800-697-3743 (in the U.S.) or 603-889-8650 for more information.

Also included on the CD is PagePlus Intro. Don't confuse this version of PagePlus with the Introductory level in PagePlus 3.0. They are

➜ PagePlus TIP
When you install PagePlus, a timer starts that gives you 60 days to work with it. This version of PagePlus can only be installed once. If, after installation, you want to purchase the product for unlimited use, see the upgrade information in Appendix D.

FIGURE 2.3 The PagePlus Install Select Options box

not the same. We will use the full version of the program PagePlus 3.0, for the lessons in this book. Many of them are created using the Introductory level. If you want to use the PagePlus Intro software included on the CD, you may do so for an unlimited time. You may want to experiment with PagePlus Intro on your own. But again, be warned that the lessons in the book do not pertain to this product.

DrawPlus 1.0 is a bonus included on the CD. This drawing program works with PagePlus 3.0 and other Windows applications through the Windows clipboard. See Chapter 17 for more information on DrawPlus.

The ArtPack collection included on the CD offers 500 Windows Metafiles, which you can use with PagePlus or any other Windows application that imports Windows Metafiles. DrawPlus, ArtPack, and PagePlus Intro can all be used for an unlimited time.

The Memory Dilemma

As described in Chapter 1, the optimum desktop publishing system that combines both affordability and practicality is a 60 MHz

Pentium or better with at least 8 MB of RAM and a 500-MB hard drive. Of course, if your budget permits, you may want to get a faster 90-MHz system with more RAM and a larger hard drive. No matter how monstrous you think your machine is, it's amazing how much memory today's graphics-intensive applications require. Your system is still susceptible to the "Out of Memory" message, which can be a little disheartening, especially if you've just purchased a PC that has 16 MB or more of RAM.

"Out of Memory" means you've run into the 1-MB "RAM wall." If you don't mind getting a bit technical here, the problem goes back to 1980 and the original IBM PC design. The first IBM PCs were designed with memory separated into two parts: a low-memory portion of 640K and an high-memory portion of 384K (for a total of 1 MB). And even though a lot has been done to overcome those limitations, for compatibility sake we still have to have all applications (both DOS and Windows) run in the memory space below 640K.

Things get even more complex when you add CD-ROM drives, sound cards, video-capture boards, and the like—each requiring their own memory-resident program (sometimes called a TSR, for Terminate and Stay Resident). In no time at all you can bog down your PC's conventional memory to the point where it won't run anything but small programs, and that's when you might get the "Out of Memory" message. But don't despair! There are solutions to RAM cram. Read on.

Types of Memory

First, it's important to understand that there are actually two main kinds of memory in your PC—ROM and RAM. ROM (read-only memory) contains the all-important BIOS (basic input/output system), the permanent program that acts as a translator between the operating system (usually DOS) and the computer hardware. As the name implies, because it's read-only it can't be changed. You do, however, need to know about it because in order for your PC to run at maximum capacity, portions of the programs in ROM get tucked into RAM. RAM (random-access memory) is the memory that stores information temporarily while you are using the computer. All programs run in RAM, and your desktop publishing creation is temporarily stored in RAM before it gets saved (more permanently) to your hard disk.

When we talk about making the most of the memory in your computer, we are talking about RAM. Although all RAM is physically the same (it exists on "chips"), it's actually handled by the BIOS and the operating system in five different ways, as conventional (sometimes called "base") memory, upper memory, extended memory, expanded memory, and the "high-memory area."

Memory Managers

When you add a CD-ROM drive, a sound card, a fax board, data compression software, and other drivers that remain resident in memory, you will find that your conventional memory quickly becomes woefully limited—or possibly used up to the point that your applications won't run at all. The latest versions of MS-DOS take up nearly 200K alone. DOS comes with a memory manager that will put DOS itself and other programs into upper memory and high memory. There are also third-party memory managers such as QEMM (from Quarterdeck), NetRoom (from Helix), and 386Max (from Qualitas). These competing companies have come up with clever and unique ways of maximizing memory. The optimizers that come with the various versions of DOS do indeed free up conventional memory, but they're conservative. And the amount of conventional memory they free up may still not be enough for a loaded desktop publishing system.

Memory and Windows

With the ability to have multiple applications open at once comes the need for better memory management when running applications (such as PagePlus 3.0) under Windows. And not only can you run multiple Windows applications at once, but you may also want concurrent access to DOS applications. Naturally, switching from Windows to DOS and from application to application uses a lot of RAM. Memory management not only gives you the conventional memory you need to run your applications, it can also result in better-performing DOS sessions under Windows.

In the next iteration of Windows, dubbed Windows95, Microsoft plans to integrate DOS and Windows into an almost-seamless whole. This doesn't mean, however, that memory management problems will disappear. Most memory management problems are caused, for the most part, by DOS applications and their need for conventional memory. While Windows95 will also come packed with virtual device drivers that don't run in conventional memory, you will get some relief from the conventional-memory drain, but not completely. Whether you move to Windows95 or not, it looks like you will always have to manage your memory.

Basic PC Maintenance

While the subject of PC maintenance can fill a book unto itself, it's important to understand a few of the most basic points before you begin using your PC as a desktop publishing machine. Keeping the system you use for desktop publishing optimized is the insurance you need to guarantee your job gets done. Proper maintenance of your system includes running diagnostics, performing backups, defragmenting for optimization, uninstalling unwanted files, caching for better performance, and compressing files to make room for more. The following is a quick guide through these maintenance basics.

DIAGNOSTICS

Diagnostic utilities are included with DOS 6.2, or they can be purchased as add-on products from companies such as Symantec, Central Point, and TouchStone. These utilities can identify and repair a variety of problems. When used regularly, you can spot potential problems before they cause you to lose your work. Many of the utilities are capable of repairing or restoring damaged or deleted files as well. In addition, many include a very important feature that you should never be without: the emergency disk. This disk stores the files you need to get up and running again in the event of an emergency. You can automatically create an emergency disk for your PC when you install the diagnostic software. Once you create it, label it with a date, and keep it close at hand.

BACKUPS

Backing up to floppy disks is impractical with today's large-capacity hard drives. A better alternative is tape backup, using tape drives. Many of these connect to the parallel port in your PC, which is the same port you plug your printer into. The beauty of a parallel drive is that it is easy to connect.

Nonparallel port drives are either internal or external and come in three varieties: one connects to a floppy controller, another connects to an IDE hardware controller, and a third type connects to a SCSI controller. Nonparallel port drives are faster than those that run through the parallel port because data transfers faster through the floppy, IDE controller, or SCSI connector. However, parallel port drives are fast enough for most desktop publishing needs, and their ease of use and convenience should certainly put a parallel port drive on your desktop publishing office must-have list.

Start by making a full backup, and keep it in a safe place. When it's time to make another full backup, use a different tape so you won't overwrite the only backup you have. Do full backups at least once a month, if not weekly. After you have a full backup, run weekly or daily incremental backups in which you backup only the data that has changed or is new since your last backup. Again, don't overwrite your last partial backup. Always keep a set of full and partial backups, and use a separate set of tapes for the backup you're currently performing.

DEFRAGMENTING

When you use your PC regularly, you open files, save them, and often change them. Each new version of the file may become relegated to various portions of the hard disk. This is called fragmentation. Getting rid of fragmentation is sometimes referred to as "defragging" or "optimizing."

Your hard drive becomes fragmented because every time you erase a file, the space is made available for storage. When you save a new file to disk, DOS puts it in the first available empty space. If there's not enough room for the whole file, part of it is put elsewhere. The longer you use your hard disk the more fragmented your files get. This means the hard disk heads have to scurry around the hard disk surface, gathering parts and pieces to construct an entire file. This takes more and more time.

To ensure that your disk stays defragmented, run a disk optimization program that puts all your files in contiguous order on your hard drive. Reorganizing the data in this way improves your system's performance, because the hard drive's head won't have to move as much to read the data.

How often you should optimize your disk depends on how much you use your PC and what types of files you're storing. For example, if you create lots of desktop publishing designs, like letters or memos, your disk can become defragmented very quickly. It takes only a few minutes to run a quick optimization, but a full-fledged optimization takes much longer—up to several hours, depending on how large your hard disk is. Try to do a complete optimization at least once a month.

CACHING

To understand what caching is, picture your system RAM as a place where data is stored, in addition to the hard or floppy drive. Caching software speeds up your PC by using part of RAM as a safe storage place for data that you access frequently. If you don't use any caching, every time you start a program or call up a document your PC has to go to the hard disk to get the files you need. The hard drive has a read/write head that has to move to the location of the data and then read it. While this can be fast enough, if the data is already in RAM, access is quick as a wink.

One caching utility comes with DOS, and you may already be using it without realizing it. The utility is called SMARTDRV, and to find out if you're already using it, check your `AUTOEXEC.BAT` or `CONFIG.SYS` files to see if you have a `SMARTDRV.EXE` line in it.

Caching is especially important for Windows users. Because of its ability to multitask, files are continually being read from and written to disk. Versions of Windows prior to Windows for Workgroups 3.11 include SMARTDRV, but if you don't want to use it you can install an add-on program or utility. Windows for Workgroups 3.11 offers its own sophisticated caching.

COMPRESSION

Even if you have the largest hard drive on the block, after creating a few desktop publishing documents and storing a few graphics files you may find that you're running short of disk space. You can unload unneeded applications, but it's more practical to compress the data that you use frequently. Microsoft includes the new compression utility DriveSpace with DOS 6.22. Other compression products are offered from companies such as AddStore, Stac Electronics, and Vertisoft Systems. Some people are wary of compression products, but this is only because of the critical functions performed by the compression software itself. Compression software must compress every bit of data on the hard disk without losing any of it. With this in mind, you can't neglect the ever-important safety measures you should take before installing or using compression software. First, make sure you have a backup of the current data on your system. Also keep your emergency disk available. Next, clean up your system, as described above, by running an uninstall utility and an optimizer. Finally, be aware of any suspected incompatibilities between the compression software you're running and any TSRs you may have loaded. Unload TSRs, if necessary.

UNINSTALLING

Windows tends to scatter bits of applications in INI (initialization) files and in other places you'd never think of looking. If you want to remove an application from your system, a lot more is involved than just deleting the icon. Using a utility designed to uninstall these applications will find any hidden bits of them, as well as any duplicate files you don't need. Utilities for uninstalling files are available from Quarterdeck, MicroHelp, Vertisoft, and other manufacturers. However, when using these products, be careful not to indiscriminately delete files just because the utility tells you to. Make sure, first, that the files are not critical to Windows or to certain applications.

When you install the 60-day version of PagePlus 3.0 from the CD, PagePlus puts different files in private Serif directories on your hard drive. Rather than searching for all the PagePlus-specific files to delete, use a utility that will do the uninstalling for you, or you can do it yourself. The software on the CD–ROM will install the following file:

```
c:\windows\serif.ini
```

and the following directories:

```
c:\windows\serifdll or c:\serif\serifdll
c:\serif\pp30
c:\serif\drawi10
c:\serif\art&bord
```

If you want to completely uninstall all the Starter Kit, delete the following file and directories (and all files contained within):

```
c:\windows\serif.ini
c:\windows\serifdll
c:\serif
```

If you simply want to delete PagePlus, delete the directories (and all files within):

```
c:\serif\pp30
```

You don't need to uninstall DrawPlus, ArtPack, or PagePlus Intro, as these products are not time-limited. You'll want to hang on to DrawPlus and ArtPack anyway, because they work with other Windows products.

Chapter 3

Design

The design of a page is as important as the text you put on it. You can write as eloquently as anyone, but if your prose is presented in a hard-to-read manner, the reader either won't read it or will quickly lose interest. This chapter touches on the elements of design, which will help move you forward and become a proficient desktop publisher whose messages get noticed.

The proliferation of personal computers, coupled with easy-to-use desktop publishing programs, has created a deluge of printed information. Every organization seems to have at least one newsletter, and the mail is loaded with self-published announcements of store sales, parties, fund-raising events, and more. The simple fact that we're increasingly bombarded by desktop-published documents is reason alone to make yours look as good as they can be. The first step is to capture a potential reader's attention, to get them to actually read your message. If you get them to look at the page, you may be more than halfway there. So design is more than just looking good on the page. It's presenting the message in an inviting way in order to capture an audience.

The downside to today's ready access to computers, desktop publishing software, and fancy printers is not just the over-abundance of written material it has created, but also the lousy designs it can produce. Just because someone has to get a message out doesn't justify a poor choice of type size, style, or color.

Being a trained graphics designer is a great advantage to the desktop publisher; however, it is not necessary to be a pro. To produce good-looking documents, there are just a few steps that you should take, which we'll go over in this chapter. Otherwise, don't fret about not having a professional graphics background. In fact, consider yourself a designer. You know what you like. When you flip through a magazine, certain ads jump out at you, and others leave you cold. If you examine the pages you like, you'll see similarities. You might like a certain typeface, a certain amount of white space, or prefer ragged over justified text. These are terms that nondesigners are not expected to know; the important thing, however, is that when you see a page you like, you know why you like it. So read on. In this chapter, you'll learn what terms like "ragged" and "justified" mean, you'll learn how to plan the "look" of a document, and you'll learn the basics of design.

Planning

In planning your document's design, you should consider four basic elements: the document's purpose, its audience, constraints placed upon the design, and the document's format.

Purpose and Audience

To begin, it's most important to understand the purpose of your document. An announcement about a new lawyer joining the firm carries a very different message than a poster about a concert in the park. These messages may have different audiences, but more importantly, they serve two different purposes. It is that purpose for which you are designing.

The purpose reflects your goal or the point you want to get across. For example, the purpose of a business card is to create an identity or an image. The purpose of an advertisement is to persuade someone to buy a product. The purpose of a calendar of events is to inform and encourage participation.

To figure out your piece's purpose, ask yourself why it is needed and who it is intended for. How much information does the audience already have, and how much do you have to hand to them? How much time will the audience spend focused on your piece? How attentive is your audience—and do you have to win their attention? By answering these questions you can decide what kind of information should be included, how it should be presented, and what it should look like. You also may want to consider the paper the document is printed on—if you're going after a certain image, make sure that image is conveyed from top to bottom.

After you've figured out the purpose or goal of your document, you can plan your design. A good starting point is to look at examples of what you like and determine what it is you like about them. Collecting several samples of documents that serve a purpose similar to your document's can be a good starting point. If you cannot find examples of documents with a similar purpose, try to sketch out a few.

Constraints

The third step in the planning process is to determine what your constraints might be. You can come up with a gloriously elaborate design, but if your software or hardware can't handle it, your printer won't print it, and you can't afford either the time or the cost of producing it, then it is out of the question. Know the constraints of your software, how the document will be output, what your time limit is, and how much you can afford to spend.

If you're producing a document for someone else, your options may be very different than if you have free rein to design anything you like. If it's a document for a corporation, there may be a corporate style you must adhere to. You may be asked, for instance, to include the corporate logo in a certain position, color, and size on the page.

Unfortunately, software constraints are often discovered as you are working on a piece and are under the pressure of a deadline. The best advice here is to only embark on a desktop publishing project under deadline if you are using tried-and-true software. Sometimes problems that appear to be software difficulties or limitations are actually due to the user's lack of experience with the software. So make sure that you know the software you'll be using, and make sure it's worthy of the job, before you commit to it.

Another constraint can be imposed by your hardware. It may not be capable of producing the document you have in mind, or it may crash midstream, taking your work with it. It's important to keep your hardware in good working condition to minimize potential surprises. PCs running Windows should be optimized and defragmented on a regular basis, and regular backups should be a part of your work routine. For more information on optimizing your PC, see the section Basic PC Maintenance in Chapter 2. Another hardware limitation you may encounter if you plan to print the document yourself, is that your printer won't handle PostScript or won't print at a resolution higher than 300 DPI. Or, you may find out that your printer doesn't have enough memory to print your document. Know your equipment before committing to the job! Often, if the problem is your printer, you can copy the job to disk and get a friend or a local print shop to print it for you on a more capable printer. (Of course, you should also make sure that the job will *fit* on a floppy disk!)

Time constraints can work both for and against you. To complete any job, most people need to have a deadline. If you're producing a document for someone else, ask them when they need it, and be realistic about whether you can accommodate their needs. If you're doing the document for yourself, give yourself a realistic deadline as well. Before you begin the project, decide how you're going to meet the deadline. Break the project into its parts, starting from the drop-dead date (deadline) for the design and the final point of the project, which is usually when you have the final documents all printed and ready for distribution. Then move backward on the time line. Find out how much time the printer requires to complete the job, and allow an extra day or two for flexibility. Keep moving back on the time line until you get to the starting date. Adjust the dates as necessary so that you've set up a realistic work schedule for yourself, taking into consideration other projects you might have under way and possible complications with the job at hand.

Cost restraints are important to know up front as well. Cost considerations can influence your decisions about many aspects of the publication, including how many colors you can use, how many pages it can be, how it will be printed, what type of paper you'll use, what type of binding, and so forth.

Format

The next step is to know what format your document will take. The format could be a book, a brochure, a magazine, a mailer, a newspaper, or some other printed vehicle. Sometimes the particular format will present you with a new set of rules to work by. Magazine advertisments, for instance, often have to meet certain size standards, and sometimes, they cannot conflict with the "look" of the publication. The format of a document can also mean it's page size or overall look.

If you are preparing a document for a client, ask them if they have an example that shows the type of format they have in mind. If the document is for a corporation, make sure you find out if you have to conform to a corporate style, which may dictate headline placement, choice of typeface, size of paper, color, and more.

When the format is left solely up to you, you have both a blessing and a curse. First you have to complete the steps listed above, so you know your purpose, your audience, and your constraints. From there you can step back and picture the finished document. If it's a newsletter, you'll need to decide the importance of each story and place them accordingly. If you're both the writer and the editor, you can adjust the length and tone of each story to your audience. If you're working with a writer or editor, you may want to make suggestions to them, at least about the length of each story relative to its placement on the page. You are the designer, and it's up to you to guide the reader's eye across the page, with the goal of capturing their attention and fulfilling the purpose of the publication.

"Pacing" is a term used in newspaper and magazine publishing; it means that complex stories are balanced with those that are less demanding to read. Pacing can also mean that text is offset by photographs and other graphics. Put yourself in the reader's shoes, and examine the flow of the document you have in mind. If the opening is dull as dishwater, either in look or content, forget about anyone's reading on. Making the pages move for your readers will go a long way toward accomplishing your goal.

Elements of Page Layout

Creating an effective design requires a basic understanding of the elements that make up a page. You don't have to be a graphics design professional to create professional looking documents on your computer. All you need is a little knowledge about what to place on a page and a few cautions about where to tread lightly. A good rule of thumb is to keep it simple. A crowded page is a clear indication that the designer is new to the craft. While a simple page

FIGURE 3.1 A design that incorporates many page elements

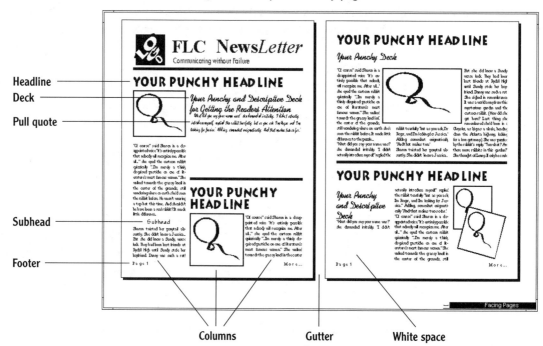

may appear too sparse, it's usually more approachable than one that is cluttered. Before you embark on creating your first page, read over the descriptions below of the basic elements of page and text layout. See Figure 3.1.

Gutter

The gutter is the space between two facing pages. When setting the gutter size, consider whether your publication will be bound, and if so, how much space you need in the gutter for binding. Most books, for example, are perfect bound, which requires at least a half-inch of white space between pages.

Columns

Columns are the vertical blocks of text in a document. Documents can have single or multiple columns. When you're deciding on column format, think of your audience and what type of information you are conveying. Multiple columns result in a narrower column width, which may be difficult to read. On the other hand, having a page full of dense text in a single column can be equally difficult to read. In addition, you can choose to have varying column widths on a page, which may serve a number of different purposes and give a striking design to your publication.

White Space

White space is space on the page that is not covered by text or graphics. Consider its placement carefully. You may want to place white spaces before and after dense text, to give the reader a break. Consider using it as a design element. Rather than loading up every available space with text or graphics, try the look of empty space and see how it works.

Boxes

Anything on a page can be boxed, but use boxes wisely. Boxes draw attention to the text or graphics contained within them; don't overuse them, or the reader won't know what is most important.

Graphics

Graphics include photographs, illustrations, clip art images, or even text used in decorative ways. Place them judiciously so they don't clutter the page. Use only those that have meaning, so you don't confuse the reader.

Elements of Text

Placing text on a page sounds like a straightforward exercise, but it isn't. Text placement should be done with much forethought—not only does it determine the readability of the piece, but it also affects the page's appearance.

Headlines

A headline (which should not be confused with a header) is the title of an article or news story.

Deck

Not to be confused with a subhead, a deck sits between the headline and the main text. Its purpose is to give more information about an article.

Subheads

Subheads are used to introduce new sections of a story and provide a snapshot of its context. Subheads serve to organize segments of text on a page. Use subheads as a graphic element by choosing a different typeface than the headline and text, but use them judiciously. As with other text elements, you can make a stronger statement by using the element conservatively.

Pull Quotes

Pull quotes are also called breakouts, callouts, or blurbs. They serve as both an informational and a graphical element. To create a pull quote, choose the most important statement on the page, and set it in large type on the page. It can be placed wherever it looks best on the page. A pull quote doesn't have to be an exact replication of the text; it can be an excerpt edited for impact.

Captions

Captions are text that explain a photograph or illustration.

Header

Don't confuse headers with headlines. Headers, also called running heads, run across the top of a publication (generally books), usually indicating the title or chapter title.

Footers

Like headers, footers (or running feet) are usually repeated on every page of a publication, but along the bottom of the page. Common footers include the chapter number, date, or page number.

Elements of Type

Like placing text, choosing type sounds simple and straightforward, but it's not. There are many varieties of typefaces, and you must choose wisely in order to capture and hold the attention of your reader.

Typeface

When you look at ads in a magazine or text in a publication, you know what you like when you see it. (Or at least you know what you don't like.) In choosing the "look" of the type on the page, it's important to be aware of what you like, but it's more important to know your audience and what will appeal to them. Age, sex, education level, and interests may indicate whether you should go with a very modern look, go the simple and traditional route, or go with something with the classical look of an earlier age.

Size

Choosing the size of type requires that you understand the importance of what the type is trying to convey. If you're creating an advertisement for the biggest sale of the year at a local car dealership, you don't want type that appears to whisper the message. You also don't want to lose the message in vast white space. When the message needs to be broadcast loud and clear, set it in large type and use up most of the available white space. If your message is more subtle, make it look that way by choosing a smaller type size and framing it with sufficient white space.

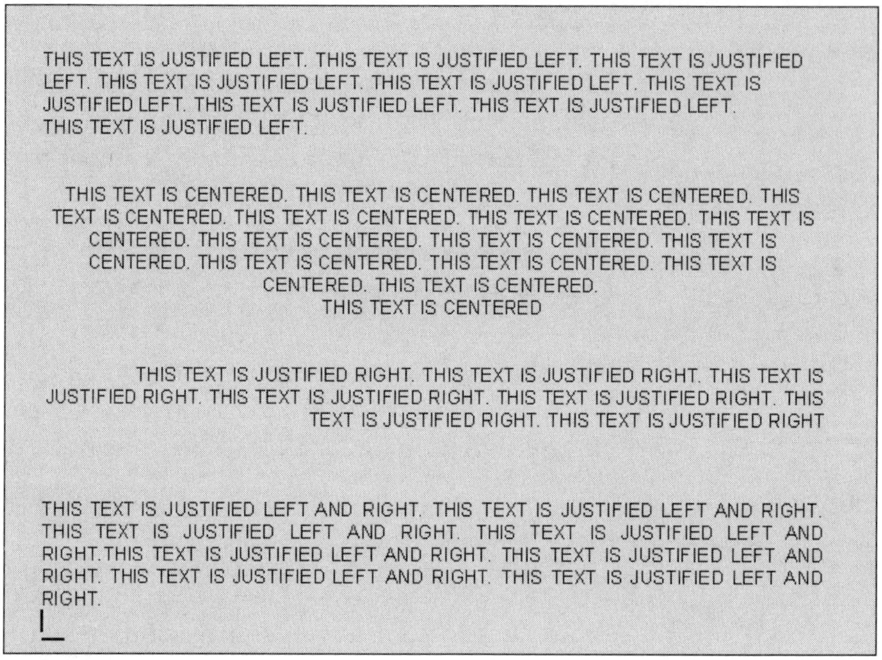

THIS TEXT IS JUSTIFIED LEFT. THIS TEXT IS JUSTIFIED LEFT. THIS TEXT IS JUSTIFIED
LEFT. THIS TEXT IS JUSTIFIED LEFT. THIS TEXT IS JUSTIFIED LEFT. THIS TEXT IS
JUSTIFIED LEFT. THIS TEXT IS JUSTIFIED LEFT. THIS TEXT IS JUSTIFIED LEFT.
THIS TEXT IS JUSTIFIED LEFT.

THIS TEXT IS CENTERED. THIS TEXT IS CENTERED. THIS TEXT IS CENTERED. THIS
TEXT IS CENTERED. THIS TEXT IS CENTERED. THIS TEXT IS CENTERED. THIS TEXT IS
CENTERED. THIS TEXT IS CENTERED. THIS TEXT IS CENTERED. THIS TEXT IS
CENTERED. THIS TEXT IS CENTERED. THIS TEXT IS CENTERED. THIS TEXT IS
CENTERED. THIS TEXT IS CENTERED.
THIS TEXT IS CENTERED

THIS TEXT IS JUSTIFIED RIGHT. THIS TEXT IS JUSTIFIED RIGHT. THIS TEXT IS
JUSTIFIED RIGHT. THIS TEXT IS JUSTIFIED RIGHT. THIS TEXT IS JUSTIFIED RIGHT. THIS
TEXT IS JUSTIFIED RIGHT. THIS TEXT IS JUSTIFIED RIGHT

THIS TEXT IS JUSTIFIED LEFT AND RIGHT. THIS TEXT IS JUSTIFIED LEFT AND RIGHT.
THIS TEXT IS JUSTIFIED LEFT AND RIGHT. THIS TEXT IS JUSTIFIED LEFT AND
RIGHT.THIS TEXT IS JUSTIFIED LEFT AND RIGHT. THIS TEXT IS JUSTIFIED LEFT AND
RIGHT. THIS TEXT IS JUSTIFIED LEFT AND RIGHT. THIS TEXT IS JUSTIFIED LEFT AND
RIGHT.

FIGURE 3.2 Type alignment

Alignment

You have three basic choices when it comes to aligning type: justified, ragged right, or centered (see Figure 3.2). But within those three choices there are many variations. Justified means the type bumps right up against the margin; you can have type justified on one side and ragged on the other. Ragged means the lines end at irregular intervals, with no words hyphenated. Type that is justified on both the right and left sides has a formal look to it. Type that is justified on the left and ragged on the right looks less formal. Centered type is the most formal of all. Again, choosing the proper alignment depends upon the message you want to convey, as well as the intended audience.

Spacing

Spacing is one way the desktop publisher can control every element on the page. You can control the amount of space between words, between paragraphs, before and after punctuation, and around all graphic elements. The spacing between words is sometimes called

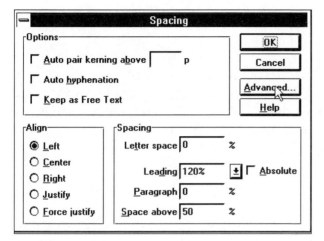
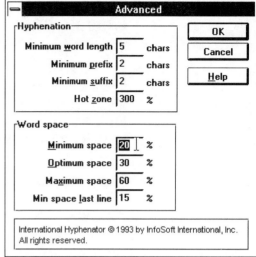

FIGURE 3.3 PagePlus spacing controls

"tracking." The tracking that is set by your desktop publishing software is usually very readable, but you may want to open up the spacing a bit for variety. Tightening up the spacing can be useful if you need to fit more text into an area, but it makes the text more dense and possibly less readable. Adjusting the word spacing is usually as simple as clicking on a few boxes, as shown above in PagePlus (Figure 3.3).

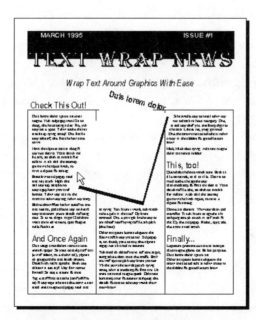

Wraps

You can wrap text around any graphic element, or even around other text, to create a highly designed look or to make efficient use of space. Like many elements of design, text wrapping should be used judiciously. See Figure 3.4.

FIGURE 3.4 Text wrapping

Graphic Impact

Breaking up the text with graphic elements enhances the overall look of the page, but graphics can serve other purposes as well. Use graphics when you need them, either to fill white space, illustrate an idea, or expand on the information in the text. Your choices for graphics are many.

Photographs

Photographs are the most realistic images you can place in your documents. The advantage of using actual photographs is that you can show exactly what or who a story is about. Like other graphical forms, photographs are a quick way to communicate. To integrate photographs onto a page you need a scanner or a CD-ROM drive with photos stored in Photo CD format. Once photos have been imported into your computer system, you can size, crop, rotate, and edit them. To do much photo manipulation, you need a software program designed to let you modify photo images, such as Picture Publisher from Micrografx.

Illustrations and Charts

Like photographs, illustrations can be scanned or imported (from drawing programs). The risk involved in using illustrations rather than photographs is that often the meaning of an illustration is open to interpretation, while a photograph's meaning is usually clear and straightforward.

Charts can be simple tables created in a word processing program or fancy "infographics" that serve to both inform and illustrate. Charts are usually computer generated and can be imported from a variety of sources into your desktop publishing program.

Clip Art

Clip art is art that is sold for reuse in publications. Today you can get clip art for just about any subject imaginable. It is often bundled

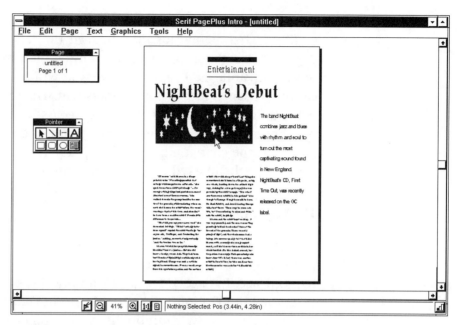

FIGURE 3.5 A publication with clip art

with graphics and design programs, but is also sold on CD-ROM disks organized according to subject category. Clip art can save you a lot of time and trouble, but it should be used judiciously—overuse of clip art can make a publication look low-budget. Clip art is also available for creating borders on publications. When used well, clip art can add pizzazz to publications. (See Figure 3.5.) The PagePlus software included with the book comes with some clip art that you can use with all your Windows applications.

Final Analysis

After you've chosen your page elements and placed them on the page, there are two ways you should look at them. One is to view them in terms of design, with an eye toward the effective use of white space and design elements. The other is to view them in terms of the quality of the writing, keeping in mind that your publication is targeted toward a particular audience. To view the overall design of your publication, you can produce thumbnails for proofing (see next section). Then, when it's time to read the text, you can print each page full size. Proofing on paper requires a few extra steps, but it has several advantages. The first is that you will be looking at the publication on paper, just as your readers will. The second is that you can mark up a proof, and even send it to a second person for further proofing. When all changes have been marked on the copy, you simply input the changes into the computer. And last but not least, you get to keep the marked-up copy to refer to in the future.

Thumbnails

To view your entire document, you can print out "thumbnail" proofs, which let you see multiple pages of your document in a reduced size. In PagePlus you can simply choose to print thumbnails from the Print Options dialog, as shown in Figure 3.6.

When you view thumbnails, you should look for how you've used white space—is there too much or too little? Look at the headers and footers and make sure they are placed consistently. Also look at the margins and gutters to ensure that they're consistent as well. And look at the overall body copy, to make sure it's not too dense or too airy. Take a good look at the text in terms of size and spacing.

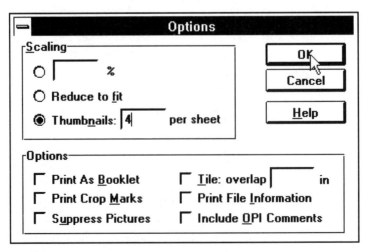

FIGURE 3.6 The PagePlus Print Options dialog

You can easily go back and subtract or add space between letters or words or lines. Also pay special attention to the spacing between paragraphs, the paragraph indenting, and the type size and weight. All of these design elements can be fine-tuned before you print a final copy.

Proofing

HINT
Read the text backwards, a word at a time, to look for typos that the spell checker didn't catch.

After you've viewed the thumbnails and either marked up elements that need to be changed or decided that the design is fine as is, it's time to proof your document. Print out a copy and proofread it. Read it once over for content, making sure that the words get the point across in the most efficient way. Read it a second time for grammar and spelling. Mark the proof up as you go along, and then go back to the computer and input the changes. Ideally, proofreading should be done by two people. Usually the best proofreader is someone other than the author. Often authors have difficulty spotting errors in their own work, or they have become so enamored of it that they don't want to change a thing.

The Next Step

We've gone over setting up a desktop publishing system, installing software, and the basics of design. The next step is to take a look at some of the specifics of desktop publishing software. The chapters that follow refer specifically to PagePlus, the desktop publishing sofware bundled with this book. But if you are familiar with or are beginning to use other desktop publishing software, many of the functions and terms will be similar. All desktop publishing software is intended to move you toward the same goal—creating documents on your computer. In the next chapter we'll look at some of the specific features of PagePlus you'll need to become familiar with before embarking on the lessons in the subsequent chapters.

Getting to Know PagePlus:
Buttons, Bars, and Other Features

Desktop publishing software allows you to create pages out of material from different sources. This material can include text from your word processor, illustrations from a drawing program, tables from a word processor or spreadsheet, or pictures from paint software or scanners. Popular desktop publishing software today includes Adobe's PageMaker, Corel's Ventura, Microsoft's Publisher, Quark's QuarkXPress, and Serif's PagePlus.

From this point on in the book, we'll talk specifically about Serif's PagePlus, although much of the language of desktop publishing is transferable from product to product. PagePlus lets you work with material from other software packages, but it also gives you the option to use Serif's add-ons. The add-ons also work with other Windows programs, so once you become familiar with the fonts in the FontPack, for example, you can use them with any of your Windows programs.

Getting Started

PagePlus is designed to meet the needs of everyone from the entry-level desktop publisher to the professional. It comes with a unique option that lets you choose to run the software in one of three levels—Introductory, Publisher, and Professional. The user interface, or what you see on the screen, is also a bit different in PagePlus than in other desktop publishing programs. The tool box and change bar include the tools you need for creating, editing, and manipulating objects. In addition to these little bars, which are chock full tiny icons, the hint line, located at the bottom of the screen, tells you what the icons mean, and the Quick Help window gives you further advice about what you've selected on the page.

Other features of PagePlus are similar to the features in other desktop publishing programs. For example, PagePlus 3.0 is an OLE (object linking and embedding) client. OLE is a technology, developed by Microsoft, that lets you share information among Windows applications. If you've created an illustration in Harvard Graphics, for example, you can embed the graphic in your PagePlus document. OLE is easy to use and requires very little understanding of the technology that makes it work. (For more information on OLE, see the on-line tutorial that comes with Windows.) PagePlus 3.0 also works with Windows fonts and uses TrueType (the standard font-scaling technology used by Windows 3.1). PagePlus 3.0 is a full-color desktop publishing program, allowing you to import and color-separate 24-bit color pictures. PagePlus 3.0 includes a word-processing program, called WritePlus, which you can use to create or edit text for your pages. Or you can choose to import text from another word processor, such as WordPerfect or Word for Windows. Finally, PagePlus 3.0 comes with templates, which are ready-made pages for you to use or modify as needed.

At this point you're probably eager to start PagePlus and begin creating some pages of your own. We'll take the process one step at a time, ensuring first of all that the software is correctly installed and that your printer is connected and ready to receive PagePlus files. To start up PagePlus, double-click on the PagePlus icon (Figure 4.1).

If PagePlus does not start, you'll need to access its Install Help. To do this you must use the Windows Help menu from the Program Manager window. Select Contents from the pull-down Help menu. Then select Open from the File menu. Make sure your PagePlus CD is in the drive, and select `install.hlp` (using whatever drive letter is appropriate). Go to the Troubleshooting: Installation section, scroll down to the section on specific problems, and see if any of the problems listed match yours. If, for example, the install program will not start, move your cursor to that line and click. You'll get handy information that will tell you that there may be something wrong with your hardware or software. You may want to reread Chapters 1 and 2 on setting up your hardware and software, or contact a technical support person to lend a helping hand. If you think the problem is caused by PagePlus, call Serif support at 603-889-8650 or fax 603-889-1127.

FIGURE 4.1
Starting PagePlus

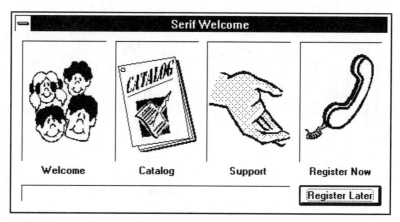

FIGURE 4.2 The PagePlus Welcome screen

Assuming that all is well, when you start up PagePlus the first thing you see is the Serif tiger, which quickly leaves the screen on its own. Then you'll see a Welcome screen (Figure 4.2), which gives you information about registration and support. Just click on OK or hit Return after you've read the Welcome information.

You can click on Catalog to find out more about Serif's products, including the add-ons mentioned in this book. Order numbers are displayed on-screen (they can also be found in the back of this book, in Appendix D). Again, click OK when you've finished reading the Catalog information.

The Support window explains Serif's mission to provide fast, friendly technical advice and support from a team of on-call experts. Again, phone numbers are listed at the bottom of the window. Click OK when you're finished with the Support window.

The Registration window gives you two simple ways to register your software. You can call the toll-free 800 number or fax your registration information to the toll-free fax number. Click OK when you're finished with this window. And to leave the Serif welcome window altogether, click Register Later.

The next thing you'll see is the StartUp Assistant window (Figure 4.3). This includes a choice of Blank Page, Templates, Publications, and Demo. It includes a box that you can check if you don't want StartUp Assistant to greet you each time you start PagePlus. Use this option with caution, however. If you tell it to go away, the only way you can get it back is to reinstall the software!

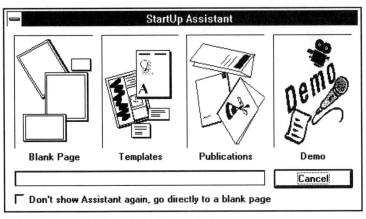

FIGURE 4.3 The StartUp Assistant window

If you click on Blank Page, you'll get the working window of PagePlus (Figure 4.4). You'll see the title bar, menu bar, and scroll bars. There are also rulers around the edge of the pasteboard area, and a status bar along the bottom. There are also three floating palettes, the tool box, which says "Pointer" in the title bar, the change bar, which says "Page" in the title bar, and the quick help box, which looks like a yellow sticky tag. We'll get back to the blank page just as soon as we've explored the other windows you see on start-up.

The second item in the StartUp Assistant window is Templates. Templates are predesigned layouts that you can use to create your own pages. See Figure 4.5.

FIGURE 4.4 The PagePlus working window

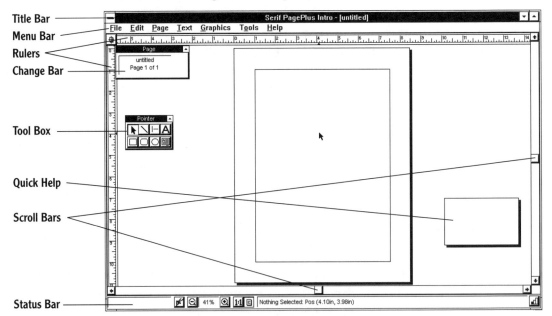

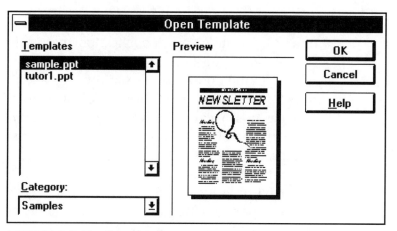

FIGURE 4.5 The Open Template window

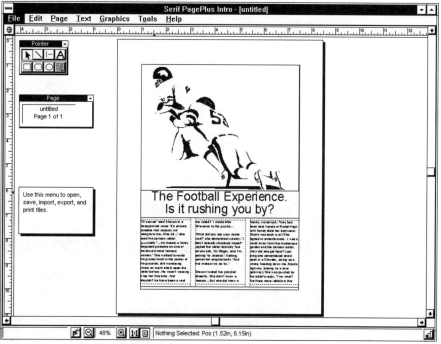

FIGURE 4.6 A PagePlus template

You can call up a template and use its design for your own publication—just change the text and graphics for an almost instant publication. You can also create your own templates and store them for future use. See Figure 4.6.

Use the File Open window to open any publication you've saved or any template or other publication that is already stored on your system. See Figure 4.7.

The Demo option in the Startup Assistant gives you a quick electronic presentation of the features of PagePlus. The opening window includes tips. You can click on the Next Tip button to see more, or check the box that tells the software to never show a tip again. You can also choose to not see a daily tip, but to see fun stuff such as cute little phrases like, "Today is the first day of the rest of your desktop publishing life . . ." If you don't tell PagePlus not to show tips, they will pop up randomly as you use the program. When you close the Tip box, the demo begins. See Figure 4.8.

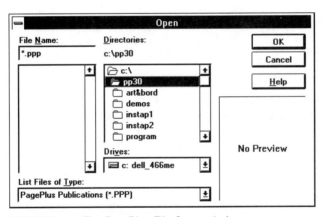

FIGURE 4.7 The PagePlus File Open window

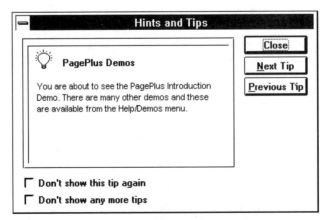

FIGURE 4.8 The Hints and Tips window

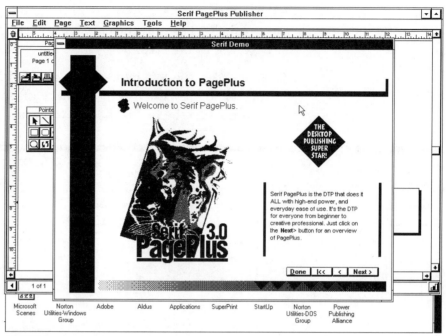

FIGURE 4.9 The PagePlus demo

You might want to scroll through the demo to get a feel for the powerful features included in PagePlus. Just click the Next button to move along through the demo. When you're done with the demo, click Done. See Figure 4.9.

A Test

In the StartUp Assistant window, click on Blank Page. Let's follow the steps below to create a simple page and try to print it out, just to make sure that all is working before we charge into full document creation.

1. Move the mouse pointer over to the tool box, to the button on the bottom left. When your mouse cursor is on this button, a label right next to the tool pops up that says Box Tool, and the quick help box tells you to use this tool to draw a box. Click on the icon with your left mouse button.

2. Your mouse cursor changes into a cross, or what is called a "crosshair." Position the crosshair on the middle of the blank page. See Figure 4.10.

3. Hold down the left mouse button and drag out a box shape. You do this by moving the mouse diagonally, releasing the button when the box is the size you want. See Figure 4.11.

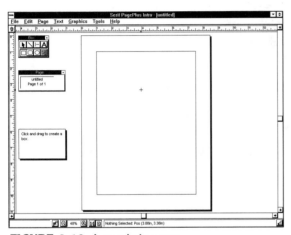

FIGURE 4.10 A crosshair cursor

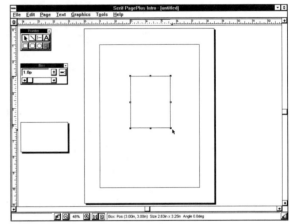

FIGURE 4.11 Creating a box

Note that a set of properties is listed along the bottom of the screen, showing the position, size, and angle of the box you've drawn. Also, the change bar has stopped showing page information and now shows information about the box you've drawn.

4. To add text, move the mouse pointer to the tool box again, but this time to the Text Tool button on the top right (Figure 4.12). Click the left mouse button.

5. The mouse cursor changes to an "I-beam." Move the I-beam to the middle of the page (Figure 4.13).

Click the left mouse button and the I-beam changes to a blinking caret, which is the text-editing cursor. You may now type a few words. You'll see that the change bar has changed to text and the status bar shows the text position, size, and angle. The text is shown very small, but by clicking on the 1:1 button in the status bar (at the bottom of the screen) you can bring it up to full-size view. See Figure 4.14.

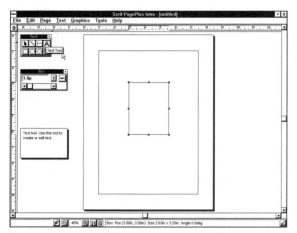

FIGURE 4.12 The Text Tool button selected

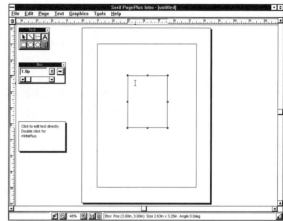

FIGURE 4.13 An I-beam cursor

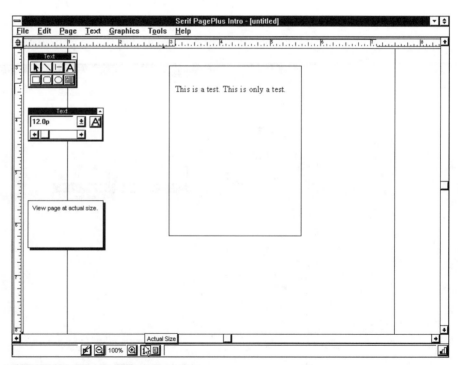

FIGURE 4.14 The actual-size view

To print the page, click on the File menu and pull it down. Then click on Print and click on OK to print. (Make sure your printer is connected to the computer and turned on.)

Choosing a Level

PagePlus is designed to be easy to learn and use. To make it simple for people who have no desktop publishing experience, there's an Introductory level. For those with some experience or who want more features, there's the Publisher level. And the highest level is Professional, which offers a lot more options at your fingertips. You can set PagePlus to whatever level you think you should begin with, and you can easily change it as you progress. The software included with this book offers you time-limited use of all three levels.

You can choose your level by clicking on Tools in the menu bar, or click on the PagePlus Level button on the far right side of the status bar, at the bottom of the PagePlus Window. See Figure 4.15.

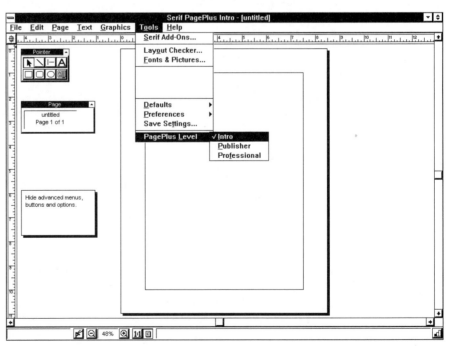

FIGURE 4.15 Changing the PagePlus levels

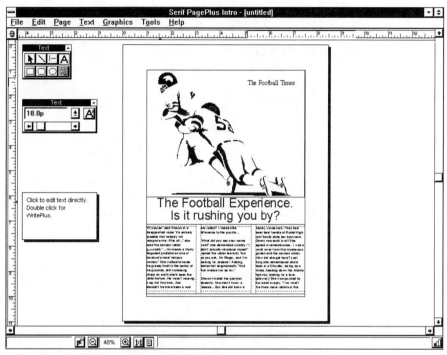

FIGURE 4.16 The Intro Level work space

INTRO LEVEL

In the Intro level, you are limited to one page and you get a slimmed-down set of tools to work with. (See Figure 4.16.) You still get the familiar Windows interface, with the menu bar, title bar, and familiar Windows buttons. If you take a look at the screen above, you'll see that you get rulers, pasteboard, and other PagePlus features that you need. We'll begin in the Intro level for our hands-on work, but you'll quickly learn that it's limited, and you'll soon want to move up to the Publisher level.

PUBLISHER LEVEL

The Publisher level adds to the Intro features, but it still gives you a helping hand. The tool box and change bar have an extra row of buttons. And the property palette lets you choose a property for the change bar to modify. You can also create more than one page with the Publisher level, so you get a page button on the status bar for moving from page to page. See Figure 4.17.

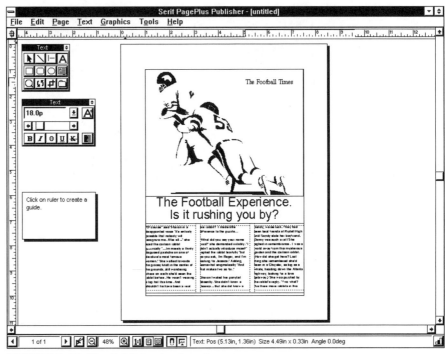

FIGURE 4.17 The Publisher level work space

PagePlus TIP
To get to the little yellow QuickHelp box back, just click on the status bar. Click on QuickHelp box to turn it off.

PROFESSIONAL LEVEL

Now we're getting serious. At the Professional level you don't get the little yellow quick help box on-screen anymore, but you do get shortcuts on the status bar for customizing the screen display and a button to access the status editor to position objects. You also get the added tools in the tool box that you get in the Publisher level. See Figure 4.18.

The Menu Bar

As a Microsoft Windows user you're familiar with the menus that run along the top of the main window. For more information on Windows menus, title bars, scroll bars, and maximize and minimize buttons, refer to the Microsoft Windows User's Guide or run the Windows tutorial from the Program Manager window.

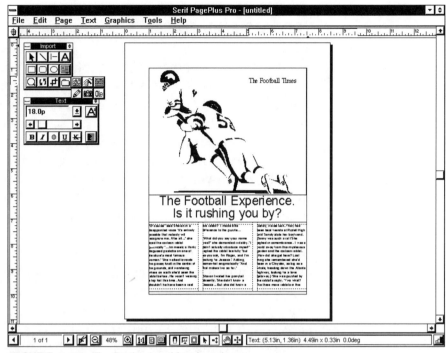

FIGURE 4.18 The Professional level workspace

In PagePlus, the menu titles let you access pull-down menus with commands to perform many of the tasks you can also perform from the change bar. You may feel comfortable altering objects on a page from the menus rather than from the change bar, although the change bar may be quicker. The items on the menu bar include File, Edit, Page, Text, Graphics, Tools, and Help. At the Intro level the items on the pull-down menus are more limited than in the Publisher and Professional levels. For example, when you pull down the File menu in the Intro level, you get many items to create a new publication, open a publication or template, save, import a picture or text, and print. In the higher levels you can do all of those, plus you can use the Revert command, which lets you revert back to a previous version of the publication. Also, you can check Autosave, you can export as a Picture, and you get information on what drive you're accessing and the name of the file that is open.

The Pasteboard

In a traditional graphic designer's office you'll find a drawing table, with scraps of type and artwork scattered around the edges. The pasteboard in PagePlus is a metaphor for that work area surrounding the page that's being designed. In the screen below you'll see bits of text on the side of the working page. These are lines of text that the designer may want to place on that page or fit elsewhere in the publication. When you print, only the work on the page is printed, not anything that is left on the pasteboard.

In PagePlus and other desktop publishing software, most of the display is taken up by the page and the surrounding pasteboard area. On the PagePlus pasteboard you'll find the tool box, change bar, and text or graphics you are getting ready to place on the page. (See Figure 4.19.) When you change pages, the pasteboard remains the same. Just like in a traditional designer's office, you can remove the page you're working on, but the text and graphics on the drawing table do not change. This is especially handy in desktop publishing, because you can quickly scroll through the pages in your publication to find the best place to put a particular graphic or bit of text.

PagePlus can produce pages up to 22 by 22 inches. In addition, it allows you to overlap an object from one page to the next, and it will be printed in its entirety (called a "bleed").

The Tool Box

The PagePlus tool box gives you the tools you need to create, select, move, and change text, graphics, and pictures. When you move your mouse cursor over a tool in the tool box, you'll see that it pops up the name of the tool, and that the name also appears in the hint line in the status bar along the bottom of the window.

If the tool box isn't showing, or if it is showing and you want it to go away, click on the Tools item on the menu bar, choose Preferences and click on General. In the General Preferences window

➡ PagePlus TIP
Use the F5 key to switch between the current tool and the previous tool you selected. This is handy when you're doing repetitive work, so you don't have to keep clicking on the tool box.

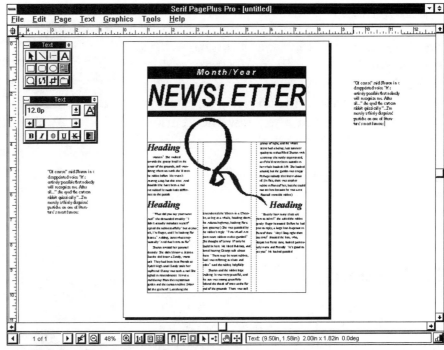

FIGURE 4.19 Text on the pasteboard

FIGURE 4.20 The General Preferences window

(Figure 4.20), click or unclick the Display tool box, as you prefer. You can also click on the close button in the upper-left corner of the tool box title bar to close the tool box.

The Title Bar

The title bar of the tool box is the bar at the top of the box. It tells you what tool is selected. You can move the tool box around on the pasteboard by clicking and dragging on the title bar. By clicking on the Show/Hide button in the upper-right corner of the title bar (Figure 4.21), you can choose to show or hide the third row of the tool box. You can only do this in the Publisher and Professional levels, because the third row doesn't exist in the Intro level.

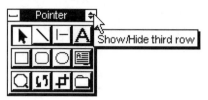

FIGURE 4.21 The tool box's Show/Hide button

The Pointer Tool

The Pointer tool (Figure 4.22) is probably the most used of all. It lets you select, move, copy, and size objects and groups of objects. It also lets you edit wrap outlines, access menu dialogs and WritePlus (the word processor within PagePlus), and create and move ruler guides.

FIGURE 4.22 The Pointer tool

The Line Tool

The Line tool (Figure 4.23) is used to create straight lines on the page or the pasteboard. To use it, select the tool and drag the mouse cursor on the page or pasteboard to create the line.

FIGURE 4.23 The Line tool

> ➡ **PagePlus TIP**
> If you want to move the line at 45-degree angles, hold the SHIFT key down while you move the mouse cursor to place the line.

The 45-Degree Line Tool

Use this tool (Figure 4.24) to create horizontal and vertical lines. Like the Line tool, you click on it and move the cursor to the page or pasteboard to create a line.

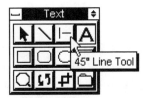

FIGURE 4.24 The 45-Degree tool

The Text Tool

The Text tool (Figure 4.25) is used to create and edit text. When you select it, the cursor changes to the I-beam. When you place the I-beam on a blank page, you can create text. When you scroll the I-beam over existing text, you can edit it.

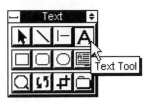

FIGURE 4.25 The Text tool

The Box Tool

The Box tool (Figure 4.26) is for creating boxes on the page or the pasteboard. To use it you click on it to select it, move the cursor to the page or pasteboard, and then click and drag the mouse to create a box.

FIGURE 4.26 The Box tool

 **PagePlus TIP**
Hold the SHIFT key down to create a perfect square.

The Rounded Box Tool

This tool (Figure 4.27) is for creating rounded boxes on the page or pasteboard. Use it the same way as the Box tool.

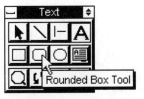

FIGURE 4.27 The Rounded Box tool

The Oval Tool

Use this tool (Figure 4.28) to create ovals on the page or pasteboard. Select the tool and drag it to the page or pasteboard to create the oval.

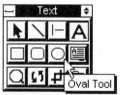

FIGURE 4.28 The Oval tool

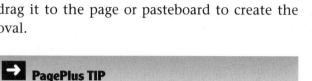

PagePlus TIP
Hold the SHIFT key down to create a perfect circle.

The Frame Tool

The Frame tool is for creating text frames on the page or pasteboard. When you select it and place a frame on the page or pasteboard, Frame Assistant pops up, giving you options for placing text inside the frame. The options let you import from WritePlus, start WritePlus, type directly in the frame, or add more frames. See Figures 4.29 and 4.30.

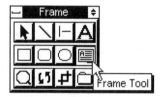

FIGURE 4.29 The Frame tool

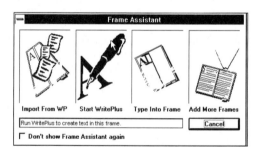

FIGURE 4.30 Frame Assistant options

The Zoom Tool

The Zoom tool (Figure 4.31) lets you zoom in or out on your work. The range of magnification is 10 to 400 percent. You can use the tool in three ways:

- Drag to fill the screen with the dragged area. Drag just a little bit, and you'll get a large magnification. Drag a lot, and you'll get a small magnification.
- Drag while you hold down the SHIFT key to fill the dragged area with the current screen, which results in decreased magnification.
- Double-click with the Zoom tool to switch the magnification between the fit-page view and the last view used.

FIGURE 4.31 The Zoom tool

The Rotate Tool

To rotate an object, click on the Rotate tool (Figure 4.32), select the object to rotate, and drag on the bottom-right handle. You can limit the rotation to 45-degree angles by holding down the SHIFT key after you've started the rotation. When you've positioned the object, release the mouse key, and then release the SHIFT key. Double-click on the rotated object to switch off the rotation.

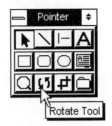

FIGURE 4.32 The Rotate tool

The Crop Tool

The Crop tool (Figure 4.33) lets you reduce the visible area of an object. To use the tool, click on it, select an object by clicking on it, then grab one of the handles and pull it inward to the desired size.

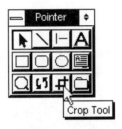

FIGURE 4.33 The Crop tool

The Import Picture Tool

When you click on the Import Picture tool (Figure 4.34), you get additional buttons added to the tool box. These are called flyout buttons, because they "fly out" from the tool box. The buttons on the flyout let you import from several of the PagePlus add-ons, including Art & Borders, TypePlus, TablePlus, DrawPlus, and PhotoPlus. The OLE button lets you import OLE objects.

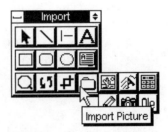

FIGURE 4.34 The Import Picture tool

The Change Bar

The change bar (Figure 4.35), like the tool box, is another floating window that contains the tools you need to manipulate a selected object. By clicking on the buttons in the change bar, you can change any object property, such as font, size, color, and more. At the Intro level to PagePlus the change bar is simplified. At the Publisher and Professional levels you get the full change bar.

Using the Change Bar

The change bar has two types of tools. One type lets you make changes that are variable, such as size of text. These are made by first picking the "property" you want from the property palette, then changing it through use of the edit window or the slider on the change bar. The property palette is the button with the large A on it. When you click on it, the palette flies out to the side, with more buttons on it. The second type of tool lets you make changes that are not variable, such as bold text. You make these changes by clicking on shortcut buttons, which are located along the bottom of the change bar. See Figure 4.36.

When you haven't selected an object, the change bar gives you a few shortcuts that let you:

- open a file   - check layout   - print
- save   - go to Help

Changes made using the change bar are made only to the object you've selected. If you make changes using the slider, the changes are not final until you click on the OK button or start a new operation. You can undo any changes you just made by clicking on the Cancel button (the X in the upper-right corner).

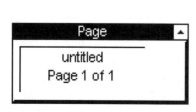

FIGURE 4.35 The change bar

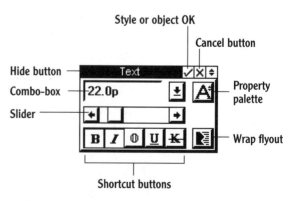

FIGURE 4.36 The change bar at work

The Hide Button

The Hide button, which is on the change bar in the upper-left corner, is for hiding the change bar. If you want to unhide it, click on Tools on the menu bar and choose Preferences/General. Then just check the change bar box to turn it back on.

The Title Bar

The title bar on the change bar is similar to the title bar on the tool box. The name in the title bar indicates what type of object is selected. Here it is text. Like the tool-box title bar, you can click on the title area and move the whole box around on-screen.

The Style OK and Object OK Buttons

On the right side of the title bar are the Style OK and Object OK buttons. The Style OK button has a red check mark in it, and the Object OK button has a black check mark. If you have a text, line, box, or oval object selected and you've made any changes with the change bar, the Style OK button is displayed.

If you click on the Style OK button, you get the AutoApply dialog, with three options. The option chosen in Figure 4.37 is *Update all objects that have this style.* Selecting this gives you a shortcut; otherwise you'd have to select three different menus and then issue the command to update. The other two choices in the AutoApply dialog are *Do not alter the style,* which is the same as clicking on the Object OK button, and *Create a new style from this object.* If you select this, you need to name the style. This is a shortcut around having to select three different menus and issue a command to create a new style.

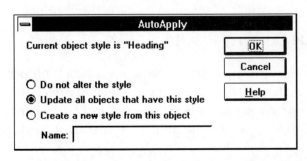

FIGURE 4.37

The AutoApply dialog

If you click on the Object OK button, you accept whatever changes you have made. The Object OK button is displayed if you move the mouse cursor over the page area. You are not tied to using this button to accept changes. If you made your selection from the menus or the tool box, PagePlus assumes you want to accept whatever changes you've made.

The Edit Window

This window is also called the combo box. It lets you select a value for the currently selected property. It's called a combo box because you can combine

- the display of the current value
- the creation of a new value
- a drop-down list of preset values

If you highlight the property that's displayed in the box, you can enter a value for the property from the keyboard. Then press Enter or click on the Object OK button. You can also click on the little arrow to the right of the value name (such as blue), and you'll get a drop-down list of values. Then you just click on the value you want. See Figure 4.38.

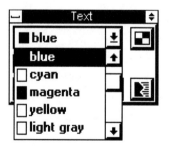

FIGURE 4.38
The combo box

The Property Palette

The property palette shows icons for each property of the object that is currently selected. You can make many changes quickly using the property palette; however, you should know that you can also make changes by using the pull-down menus at the top of the window.

If text is currently selected, icons on the property palette control:

- style
- color
- shade
- pattern
- font
- size
- width

- slant
- alignment
- leading
- letterspace
- advance (position above or below the baseline)

If graphics are selected, icons on the property palette control:

- style
- line color
- line shade
- line type
- line weight

- line pattern
- fill color
- fill shade
- fill pattern
- corners

If pictures are selected, the icons on the property palette are identical to those for a graphic, with three additions:

- picture color
- picture shade
- information (about picture type and source)

If frames are selected, the icons on the property palette are identical to those for a graphic, with the addition of an information icon that shows the position of the frame in its frame sequence and the name of the story that uses the frame.

When you click on the Property Palette button on the change bar, the property palette flies out to the side. When you click on one of the palette's property buttons, the property pops up and the palette goes away. If you don't want the palette to disappear, you have to "tear off " the palette, which we'll get to in a moment. To change the attributes of any property, double-click on any of the property buttons.

To "tear off" the property palette, which leaves it visible even as other dialogs pop up, you simply drag on its title bar.

The Slider

The slider is used to automatically change the value of a property. For example, if you want to change a font size, you select the text, then choose Size from the property palette and move the slider from right to left to decrease the size (or left to right to increase it). What's easy and fun about the slider is that you can watch the changes being made. In the case of text size, you can see what fits and stop using the slider when you've gotten it right. The arrow buttons at either end of the slider gives you finer control.

Shortcut Buttons

The bottom row of the change bar (in the Publisher and Professional levels) consists of shortcut buttons. These changes depend on the type of the currently selected object. Double-click on any of the shortcut buttons to get the dialog connected with your selected object. For example, when you select text, the shortcut buttons apply to text properties; the Character dialog pops up when you double-click on any of the buttons. See Figure 4.39.

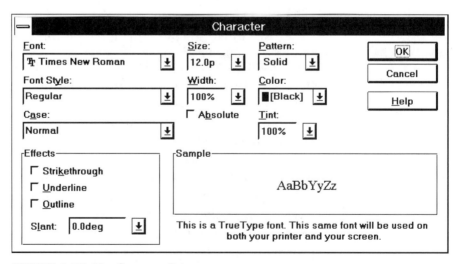

FIGURE 4.39 The Character dialog

The Wrap Palette Button

The Wrap Palette button gives you shortcuts for arranging overlapping objects. When you click on the Wrap Palette button, four wrap buttons fly out. See Figure 4.40.

The first button is the Wrap Off button. If you click it, text will not wrap around any object. If you double-click on it, you get the Wrap Settings dialog.

The second button is the Wrap Text button, which lets you wrap text around or inside an object. Again, double-clicking will get you the Wrap Settings dialog.

The last two buttons are the Front and Back buttons. If you click on the Front button, you send text (or whatever the selected object is) behind overlapping objects. If you click on the Back button, you bring the selected object to the front.

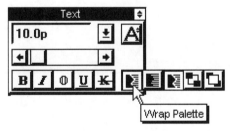

FIGURE 4.40
The Wrap Palette flyout buttons

Moving Right Along

In this chapter you've familiarized yourself with the buttons, bars, and other important features of PagePlus. You'll become very familiar with all of these as we progress through the book. The next chapter will get you going with placing boxes and text on a page, and we'll take a look at using templates, using WritePlus, and saving your work. Take a deep breath and get ready to enter the world of desktop publishing.

5

Setting Up a Page

Now that you're fully versed in the buttons, bars, and other features of PagePlus, let's put some of that knowledge to use. The goal of this chapter is to set up a page. First make sure that you've selected the Intro level. We'll start out at the simplest level because it's better to get used to PagePlus in its most slimmed-down form. Later in the book we'll get into some projects that use features from the higher levels. But for now, we'll keep it simple.

Starting from Scratch

There are basically two ways to set up a page. One is to make use of the templates that come with PagePlus. The other is to do it yourself. When you use a template, you can flow new text and resize any element, but the basic design is done for you. This is a good way to work, but it won't teach you how to do it yourself. So, for now, let's strike out on our own.

Before we start, make sure that PagePlus is up and running and you are looking at the blank page on-screen. Your screen should look like Figure 5.1.

Placing a Box

The first thing we'll do is place a box on the blank page. Follow these three steps:

1. Move your mouse pointer to the tool box and click once on the Box tool. See Figure 5.2.

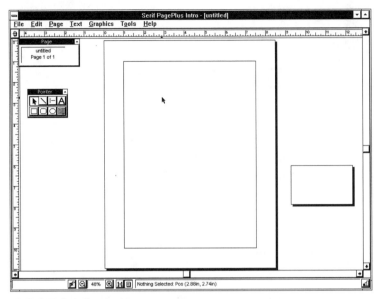

FIGURE 5.1 Beginning a new page

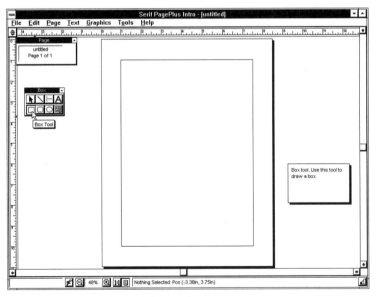

FIGURE 5.2 Selecting the Box tool

2. With the Box tool selected, move the mouse over to the blank page. (You don't need to drag it.) The mouse cursor is now a crosshair. See Figure 5.3.

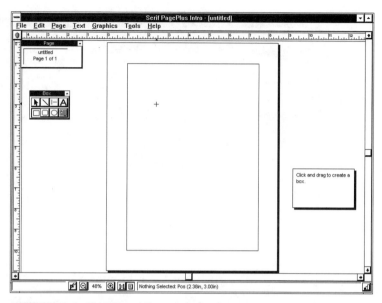

FIGURE 5.3 The Box tool's crosshair cursor

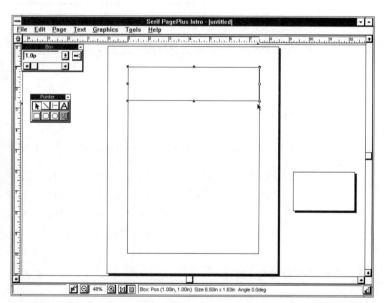

FIGURE 5.4 A newly drawn box

➡ PagePlus TIP
The small black squares around the corners of the box are called handles. To resize your box, move the mouse pointer directly over one of them; it will turn into an arrow. Click on the handle and drag it in or out, depending on whether you want the box smaller or larger.

3. Hold down the left mouse button and move the crosshair diagonally across the page. This will draw a box. When you let go, you'll see something like that shown in Figure 5.4.

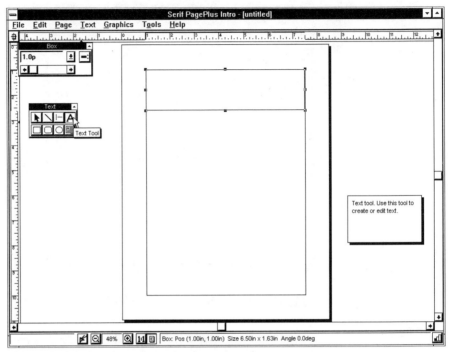

FIGURE 5.5 Selecting the Text tool

Placing Text

1. First, select the Text tool from the tool box. See Figure 5.5.

2. Place the mouse cursor where you want the text to begin. You'll see that the pointer has turned into an I-beam, with a blinking caret showing you where your text will begin. Release the mouse button and type the text!

Resizing Text

PagePlus TIP
Don't worry about what the text looks like at this point. You'll have plenty of opportunities to change the size, font, placement, and more.

1. To change the size of your text, place your mouse cursor at the beginning of it, and then click and drag across it. The text will be highlighted as shown in Figure 5.6.

2. Move your mouse pointer to the change bar and click on the slider as shown in Figure 5.7.

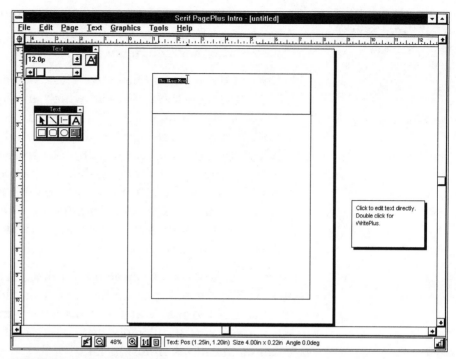

FIGURE 5.6 Highlighting text

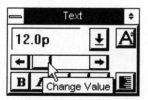

FIGURE 5.7 Changing highlighted text

3. Move the slider to the right to increase the size of the text. Look at the text in the box, and let go of the mouse button when you're satisfied with the size. You'll then see a box with a check in it on-screen. Just click the mouse button to OK the change.

Editing Text

1. Let's enter some free-flowing text to the body of the document, just for practice. To get text into a PagePlus document, you have a choice of either typing the text into PagePlus,

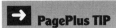

PagePlus TIP
If you want to start WritePlus, double-click on the text or click on the WritePlus button on the status bar.

importing the text from WritePlus, or importing the text from your favorite word processor. For the sake of this lesson, let's just start typing. See Figure 5.8.

2. To edit the text, you have two choices. One is to click on the 1:1 button on the status bar, which enlarges the text so that you can read it (and edit it) in PagePlus. The second choice is to call up WritePlus. Just double-click on the text and WritePlus should pop up with your text. Using WritePlus at the Intro level doesn't give you a spell checker, so you should check your work and make any modifications at this time. When you're done, double-click on the close box in the upper-left corner of the WritePlus window and you'll pop back to your PagePlus page.

Congratulations, you've created your first publication! While this first lesson has been very rudimentary, you did use many of the PagePlus features available at the Intro level. And as simple as this was, it actually gets simpler! By using the provided templates, you can create publications almost instantly.

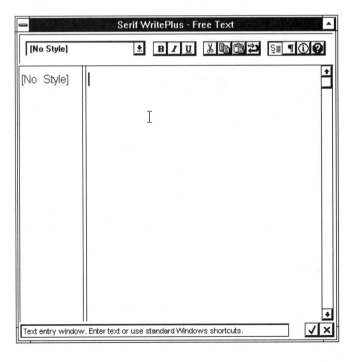

FIGURE 5.8
WritePlus text entry window

Using WritePlus

WritePlus is the word processor that comes with PagePlus. At the Intro level you get basic writing functions, plus a few added features such as a word and character count function. At the Professional level it includes spell checking, a thesaurus, find and replace functions, and a word and character count function.

Starting and Closing WritePlus

There are several ways to start WritePlus. The most obvious is to click on the WritePlus button on the status bar in PagePlus. But one of the most useful ways is to double-click on any text on a PagePlus page. You can also start WritePlus from the Frame Assistant or the Add-Ons Assistant windows.

To close WritePlus, click the buttons at the bottom-right corner of the window or use the standard close button on the upper-right corner. When you click on the close box, you are asked if you want to update or abandon changes.

After you've made changes, if you want PagePlus updated, click on the green check mark, which is the Accept Changes button. To get out of WritePlus without making any changes in PagePlus, click on the red X mark, which is the Cancel Changes button.

Features of WritePlus

WritePlus includes a yellow hint line at the bottom left of the WritePlus window. As you move the mouse around WritePlus, you get a description for each area. You also get a tool hint for each button on the WritePlus tool bar, just like in PagePlus.

Text Creation and Editing

Before working with text in PagePlus, click on the Text tool in the tool box. To change specific text in PagePlus, click on it and drag the mouse cursor across it to highlight it. If you want to change the text, you can type over highlighted text to replace it with new text. If you want to insert new text, click the cursor where you want to insert the text, and type the new text.

To end a line at a specific place without creating a new paragraph or inserting blank lines, just press Ctrl and hit Return.

Once you have a series of text blocks that form a story, you may need to move a block from one place to another. You can do this by using the Cut, Copy, and Paste commands in WritePlus. Click on Cut to cut a highlighted text block. Then choose Cut and Paste, which move it to the Windows clipboard and then to the area in PagePlus that you specify. You can also use the Cut, Copy, and Paste functions to move text to other Windows applications.

If you need to get a quick count of the words in your publication, click on the Word Count button in WritePlus (Figure 5.9). This button will pop up an Editing Story window that gives you the number of words and characters. You can also use this window to change the name of the story, which gets stored in PagePlus so that you can quickly call it up again in the future for editing.

FIGURE 5.9

The WritePlus Word Count button

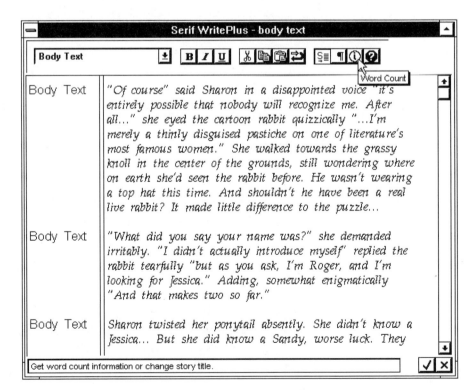

Free Text and Frame Text

Free text is text that is placed directly on a page, rather than in a text frame. It's usually used for small blocks of text, such as headlines. When you double-click on free text, it will let you edit that block of text. To resize free text blocks, click on the text and drag it to a different width. Also, using the Pointer tool, you can drag on specific handles to accomplish desired effects:

- *Top handles.* Drag these to change the vertical start position of a block.

- *Side handles.* Drag these to change the width the free text block wraps into.

- *Bottom middle handle.* Drag this to modify the leading inside the block.

Frame text is text that is flowed into columns. PagePlus flows frame text blocks into a layout established by column guides. When the frame text blocks are flowed, they are moved and resized, so their position and width correspond to the layout. Frame text blocks can be linked into a sequence of frame objects; a series of frame text blocks is called a story.

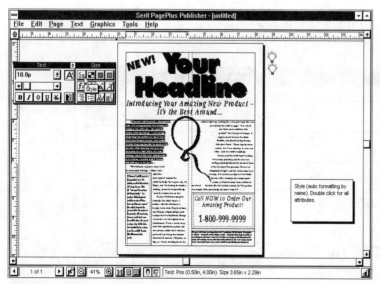

FIGURE 5.10 The Style button

PagePlus Styles

To set styles in PagePlus, switch to a higher level than Intro. Styles are most easily changed by using the Style button on the change bar. Click on the Style button on the change bar flyout. See Figure 5.10.

Double-clicking on the Style button gives you the Style Palette dialog for whatever object you've selected. In this case, it's the Text Style Palette dialog. Select the name of the style you want, or choose to create a new style. If you want to create a new style, click the appropriate box and you'll get a Style Palette dialog with a place to type in the new style name. Then you have to click to change character attributes, spacing and alignment, or tabs and indents. See Figure 5.11.

When you click on an attribute you want to change, you get the appropriate dialog box. For example, the Character dialog lets you change font, font style, case, size, width, and more. See Figure 5.12.

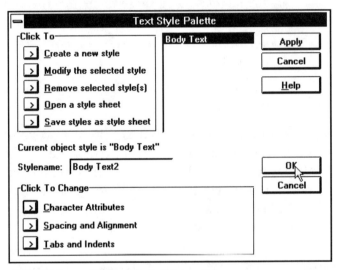

FIGURE 5.11 The Text Style Palette dialog

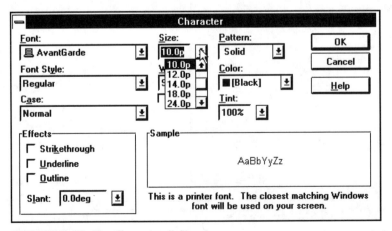

FIGURE 5.12 The Character dialog

By allowing you to assign names to styles (like "body text"), PagePlus lets you quickly apply a consistent style to different objects, whether text or graphics, without using several formatting commands. You can name a style, and later update it, thus updating all the objects in a publication that use that style. You can also save styles as "style sheets," so you can reuse them in other publications.

Find & Replace and Spell Checking

To access these WritePlus functions you have to be in a higher level than Intro. Clicking on the Find & Replace button on the WritePlus button bar pops up the Find & Replace dialog. If you want to replace a word throughout your publication, type in the word you want to find and the word you want to replace it with. Then click Find Next. The program lets you choose to replace the word one instance at a time, or all at once throughout the entire publication. If you just want to find a word, type in the word to find and click Find Next. See Figure 5.13.

To check the spelling in a publication, click on the Spell Check button on the WritePlus button bar. When you click it you get the Check Spelling dialog. See Figure 5.14.

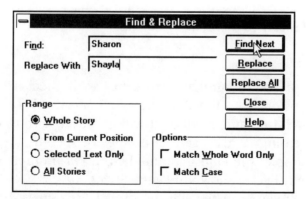

FIGURE 5.13 The WritePlus Find & Replace dialog

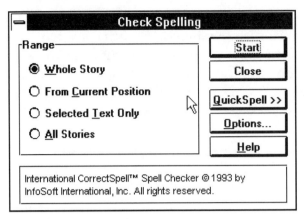

FIGURE 5.14 The WritePlus Check Spelling dialog

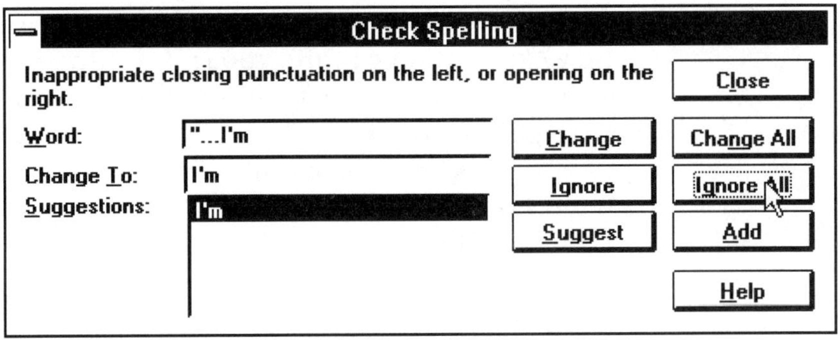

FIGURE 5.15 A spell checker response

> **HINT**
> Beware of the changes suggested by the spell checker. Always read over the suggested changes carefully before letting the spell checker change your writing. Your computer and spell checker may be smart, but your own understanding of language is far more complex!

If you're familiar with other spell checkers, you'll quickly get accustomed to the WritePlus spell checker, because it works in very much the same manner. It will go through your text and pick up on anything that is against its rules of spelling and punctuation. For example, the ellipsis points before *I'm* prompt the response in the spell checker shown in Figure 5.15.

If you want the ellipsis points left where they are, choose Ignore. On the other hand, if you want to abide by the spell checker's rules, choose Change or Change All. In most cases the spell checker will suggest changes for you to make.

Starting from Templates

Templates are precreated publications provided for your use. You may use them in several ways. One way is to use the page layout provided. You may not be comfortable designing your own pages, or you may find that the templates that come with PagePlus are just what you need. You may also like the graphics that are included with the PagePlus templates. You can also replace any of the elements on the templates with your own objects.

When you use a PagePlus template, the original is always stored intact. That way, you can open a template any time and it will always be the same. When you alter a template, save it with a new file name.

PagePlus templates are based on an 8½- by 11-inch paper size, with a ½-inch margin all around, which gives you a page area of 7½ by 10 inches. You can change that size by moving the margins, or you can change the paper size altogether.

 HINT

Adobe PageMaker, Corel Ventura, Microsoft Publisher, and other desktop publishing programs include easy-to-use templates for advertisements, greeting cards, newsletters, and more.

Using the Supplied Templates

Let's take a look at a template that comes with PagePlus and alter it to meet our needs. If you need to create a simple newsletter, you can choose the newsletter template and change elements of it to add your own personal touches.

1. To open a template, click on Templates in the StartUp Assistant window. (Call up StartUp Assistant by selecting New in the File pull-down menu.) See Figure 5.16.

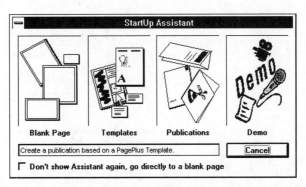

FIGURE 5.16

Accessing the PagePlus templates

2. Select a Template from the list in the Open Template dialog. Here we chose the `sample.ppt`. See Figure 5.17.

3. The template you selected will pop up in PagePlus. See Figure 5.18.

4. To alter text, select the Text tool from the tool box and highlight the text you want to change. See Figure 5.19.

5. Type in the new text. As you type, the new text will take the place of what's already there. Or you can double-click to pop

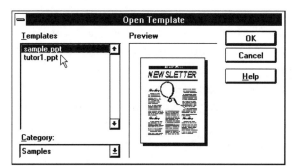

FIGURE 5.17
Choosing a template

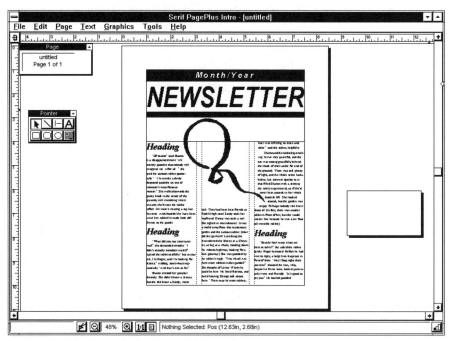

FIGURE 5.18 The sample newsletter template

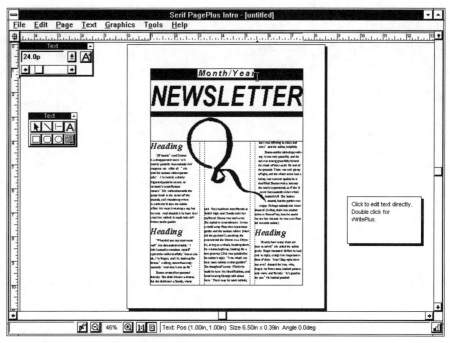

FIGURE 5.19 Selecting the Text tool

into WritePlus. There you have the advantage of maintaining the text style. In our example, the old text was replaced with new text, but the text style remains the same as on the original template. See the style list running down the left side of the WritePlus window for other style choices. See Figure 5.20.

6. When you're done in WritePlus, click the close box and you'll be asked whether you want PagePlus updated. Click Yes and you'll return to the PagePlus window with your new text in place.

Congratulations! You've created a one-page newsletter quickly and easily using a sample template!

Saving Your Work

One of the most useful bits of advice for any computer user is "save often." It's when you're busy cranking out new creations that you forget to save, and then you take the chance of losing a whole day's work or more. To save anything in PagePlus, click on File in the

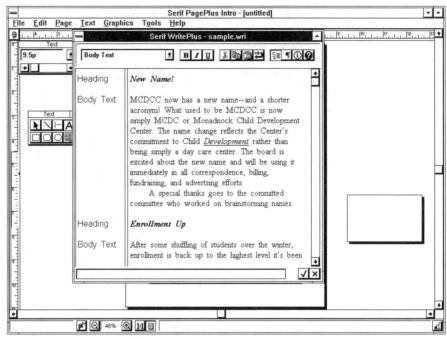

FIGURE 5.20 The WritePlus text style list

> ➡️ **PagePlus TIP**
>
> In the Professional level of PagePlus is an autosave feature, which you click on or off by clicking on Autosave in the File menu. You can also set specific time intervals so your work will be saved every two minutes for whatever time interval you choose.

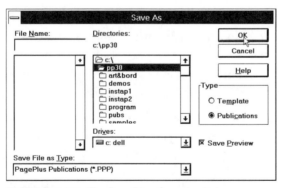

FIGURE 5.21 The PagePlus Save As dialog

> ➡️ **HINT**
>
> Save your work to a floppy disk (if it will fit) as well as on your hard disk. If the application crashes, which it can do, you'll at least have your creation saved. If PagePlus does crash, it may be able to recover your work, but it isn't foolproof. Be smart and save often, both to the hard drive and to a floppy. Some desktop publishers even store their creations on a separate hard drive.

menu bar. Then click on Save As and you'll get a dialog that lets you save your current creation in whatever directory you select. PagePlus fills in the extension to your filename automatically, so you don't have to worry about that. The most important thing is to develop the habit of saving your work at regular intervals—and give your files meaningful names so you can remember them!

Hands On

In this hands-on section you'll have an opportunity to do ten projects while following along with the lessons in the book. Using the CD-ROM-based software that's included, you can follow along with the easy steps outlined here. The lessons start out at the Intro level and assume very little desktop publishing knowledge. As you progress, the lessons build on the knowledge you've gained, and they move along through the Publisher and Professional levels of PagePlus. Because the later lessons assume that you're gaining desktop publishing knowledge as well as a familiarity with PagePlus, you won't see as many of the rudimentary screen shots. But in the first lesson, in Chapter 6, each step is explained in full detail, along with the accompanying screen shot for each move you'll make through the software.

Come along for our journey through the details of desktop publishing creation. Feel free to skip around through the lessons, but understand that some of the later lessons won't provide the hand-holding you'll find in Chapter 6 and the other early chapters.

6

Create a Postcard

Now we'll get down to the fun of actually creating publications. We'll start out slowly and simply. In this first lesson, we'll create a simple postcard. This lesson is done entirely at the Intro level of PagePlus and includes an imported graphic object and text wrapping. This is a very quick and easy method for creating a postcard from scratch, which means that we won't use a template. There are, of course, numerous ways to accomplish the same task, but this is one quick and easy method for creating a professional-looking 6- by 4-inch post card that will impress your friends and customers.

Setting Up the Page

1. With PagePlus up and running, click on Blank Page in the StartUp Assistant window as shown in Figure 6.1. (For more information on how to start PagePlus and get to StartUp Assistant, see Chapter 4.)

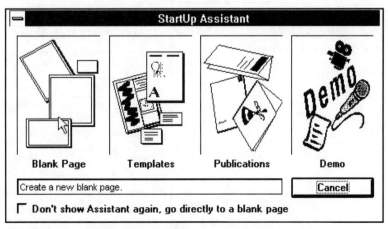

FIGURE 6.1 Opening a blank page

2. With the blank page before you, pull down the Page menu, scroll down to Page Setup, and then click on Size. Under Size, click on Custom. See Figure 6.2.

3. In the Page Setup dialog, set the page size to the dimensions of a postcard. Here we've set it to 4 inches high by 6 inches wide, and have set the margins to 1½ inches at the top and bottom and 1¼ inches on the sides. Click on "wide" instead of "tall." The term "wide" means the same as "landscape" view, and "tall" is the same as "portrait." See Figure 6.3.

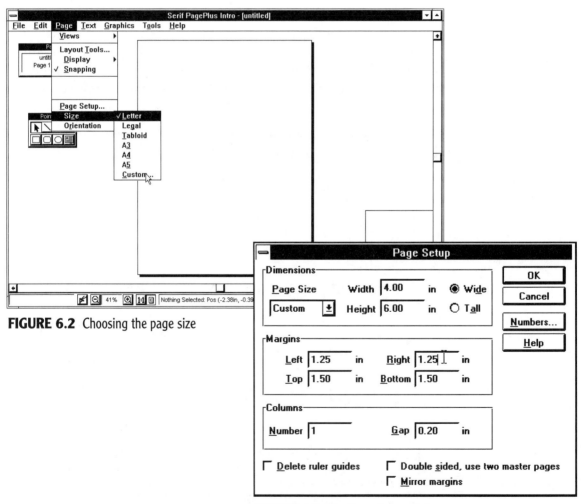

FIGURE 6.2 Choosing the page size

FIGURE 6.3 The Page Setup dialog

4. When you click OK in the Page Setup dialog, you'll see a 6- by 4-inch blank page. See Figure 6.4.

Placing a Graphic

1. To place a graphic on the page, click on File and then click on Import Picture. See Figure 6.5.

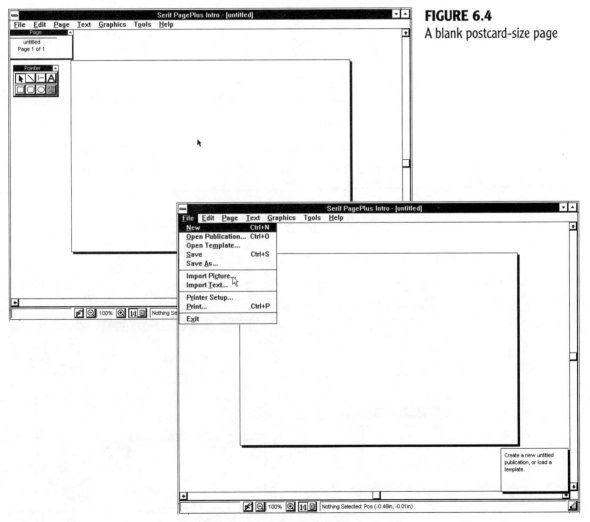

FIGURE 6.4

A blank postcard-size page

FIGURE 6.5 Importing a graphic

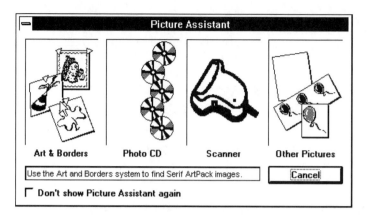

FIGURE 6.6
Choosing Art &
Borders

2. Up pops Picture Assistant (Figure 6.6), from which we'll select Art & Borders, which contains clip art files.

3. After you've clicked on Art & Borders, click on Category, and then select the picture of your choice. Here we'll click on the Natural World category (Figure 6.7).

4. Then we chose the **paws.wmf** clip art file. Notice that you can preview the clip art you've selected in the preview window. See Figure 6.8.

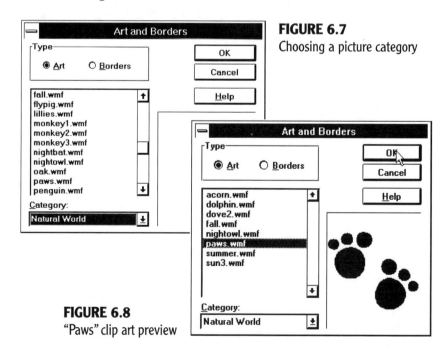

FIGURE 6.7
Choosing a picture category

FIGURE 6.8
"Paws" clip art preview

5. The cursor turns into the OLE tool, which lets you create a box on the page for the graphic. The box will not show, but it will be there, in the background, to let you move and resize the graphic at any time. See Figure 6.9.

Placing Text on the Page

1. Select the Text tool from the tool box and move the cursor to the page. See Figure 6.10.

2. Type in whatever text you want. The location is not important, as you can change it later.

FIGURE 6.9
Placing a graphic on the page

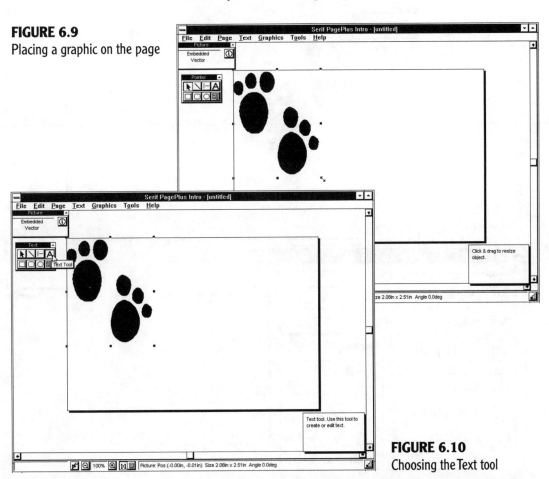

FIGURE 6.10
Choosing the Text tool

Wrapping the Text

1. Select the Pointer tool from the tool box and click on the graphic to select it. You'll see eight small handles around the border of the graphic, indicating that it is selected (Figure 6.11).

2. Click on the Tools menu and click on Wrap Settings. Click on Wrap Outside, as shown in Figure 6.12, and click OK.

FIGURE 6.11 Selecting the graphic

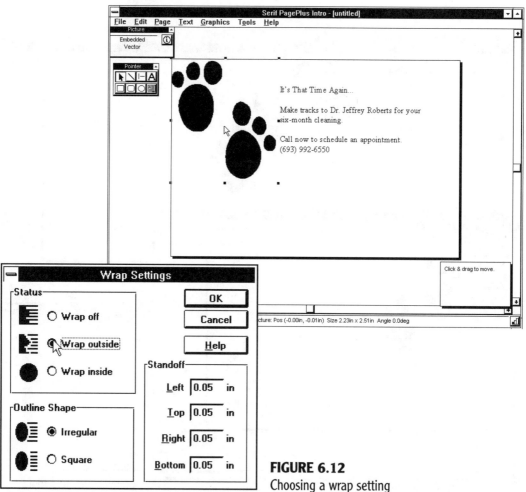

FIGURE 6.12
Choosing a wrap setting

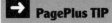 **PagePlus TIP**
You can change the size of the text with the change bar. Click to accept the change when you're satisfied with the size of the text.

3. The graphic is now ready to have text wrapped around it (Figure 6.13).

4. Select the Text tool and, holding down the left mouse button, run the I-beam over the text to select it (Figures 6.14 and 6.15).

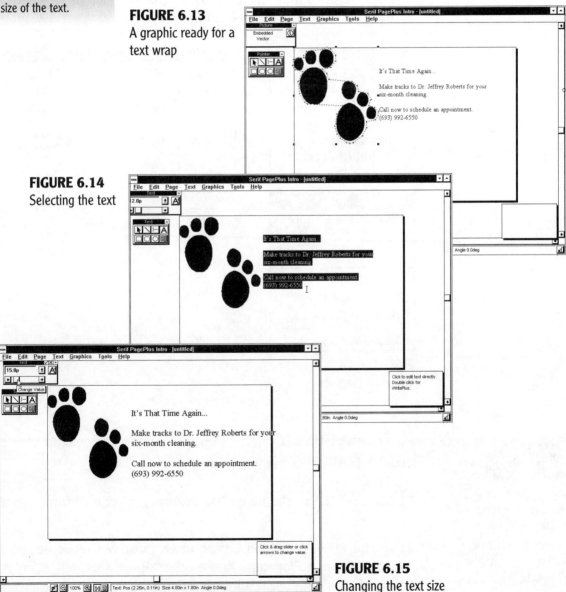

FIGURE 6.13
A graphic ready for a text wrap

FIGURE 6.14
Selecting the text

FIGURE 6.15
Changing the text size

5. Again, select the text, click on Tools in the menu bar, click on Wrap Settings, and then click on Text Will Wrap and click OK. (This is the command that performs the wrap.) See Figure 6.16.

6. Add whatever finishing elements you want.

7. Save your work by choosing Save As from the File menu and inserting a unique filename. In Figure 6.17 we've saved it as Dentist.ppp to the pubs subdirectory.

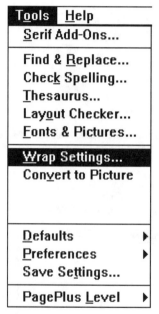

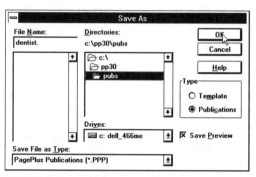

FIGURE 6.17 Naming the file

FIGURE 6.16
Wrapping the text

→ **HINT**
You can use specialty papers that are designed for printing postcards. Avery's #5389 lets you print two postcards to a sheet in your laser printer.

Printing Your Work

1. Click on File in the menu bar, and then click on Print (Figure 6.18).

2. In the Print dialog box, type in the number of copies you want to print. You can choose other options as well, such as printing at a higher resolution (Figure 6.19).

3. Click OK, and voila! Out of the printer comes your finished
   work (Figure 6.20).

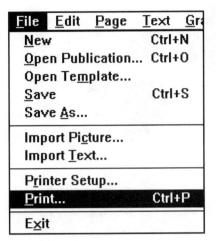

FIGURE 6.18
Choosing Print from the File menu

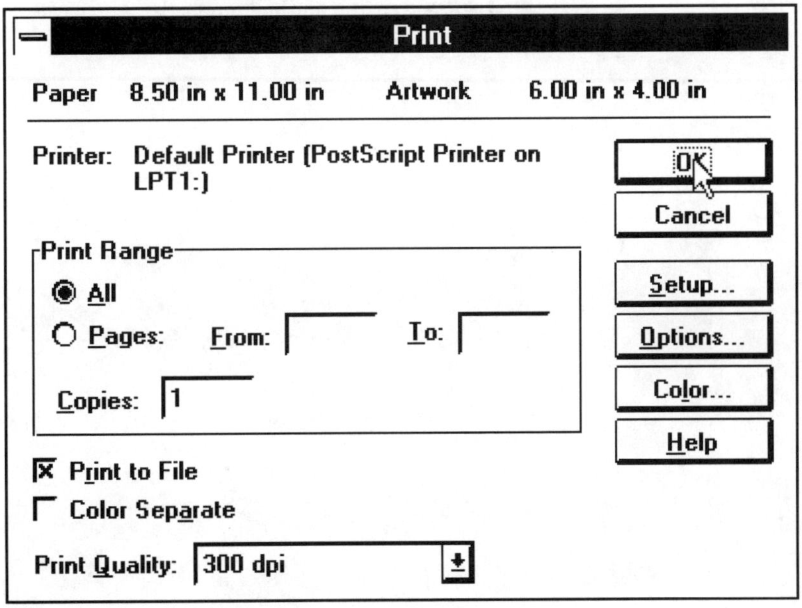

FIGURE 6.19 The Print dialog box

FIGURE 6.20 The finished product!

Create a Ticket

This is a simple lesson in creating a ticket. It's done entirely at the Intro level of PagePlus and involves creating a text frame, using WritePlus, and importing clip art. You'll be the star of your fund-raising effort when you show them the professional-looking ticket you can create!

Setting Up the Page

1. With PagePlus up and running, click on Blank Page in the StartUp Assistant window.

2. With the blank page before you, pull down the Page menu and click on Display. See Figure 7.1. Make sure Ruler and Frame are enabled (by clicking them on if they are off). This will display the ruler along the top and left margin, so you can size the ticket. See Figure 7.2.

 **PagePlus TIP**
You can't use the Page/Size menu for anything less than 3 inches.

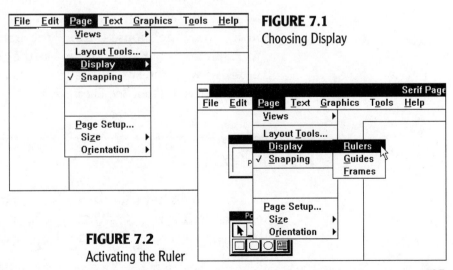

FIGURE 7.1
Choosing Display

FIGURE 7.2
Activating the Ruler

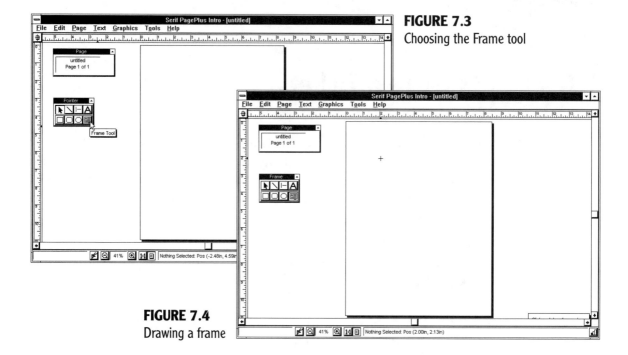

FIGURE 7.3
Choosing the Frame tool

FIGURE 7.4
Drawing a frame

3. Click on the Frame tool in the tool box. See Figure 7.3.

4. Position the mouse cursor where you want to begin drawing the frame on the page. Notice that the cursor has changed to a crosshair. Drag the crosshair across the page to create a frame the size you want for the ticket (using the rulers as a guide). You'll see the frame being created as you draw. When you let go of the mouse button, the frame will be in place, and Frame Assistant will pop up on the screen. Don't be too concerned with the size of the frame you've created. You can always change it later. See Figure 7.4.

Placing Text

1. The Frame Assistant window gives you a choice of what to do next. Let's insert text directly into the frame using the PagePlus word processor. To do this, click on Start WritePlus. See Figures 7.5 and 7.6.

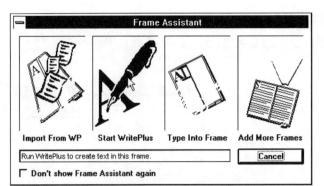

FIGURE 7.5
Accessing WritePlus

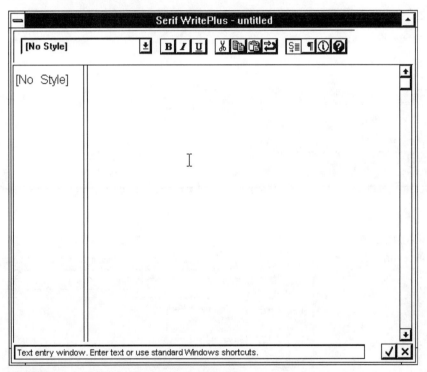

FIGURE 7.6 The WritePlus text entry window

2. Insert the text you want on the ticket. Don't be too concerned about spelling or even word choice. You can always go back and change it later. See Figure 7.7.

3. Click on the Accept Changes button. You'll pop out of WritePlus, and your text will automatically transfer to the frame you've created. See Figure 7.9.

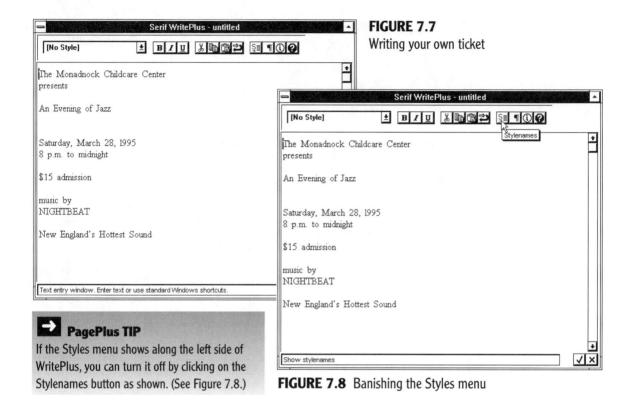

FIGURE 7.7
Writing your own ticket

FIGURE 7.8 Banishing the Styles menu

→ **PagePlus TIP**

If the Styles menu shows along the left side of WritePlus, you can turn it off by clicking on the Stylenames button as shown. (See Figure 7.8.)

FIGURE 7.9
Accepting your text

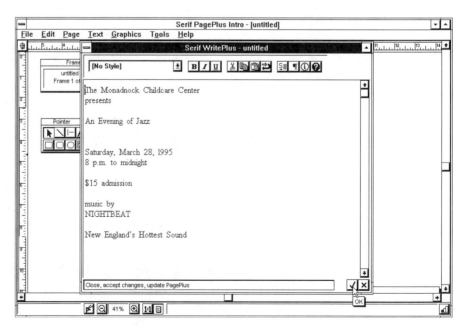

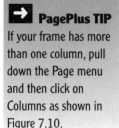
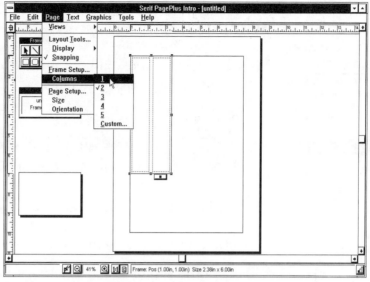

FIGURE 7.10 Setting the number of columns

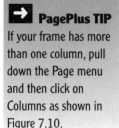

4. To edit the text or change the text style, click on the 1:1 button to bring it up to actual size. See Figures 7.11 and 7.12.

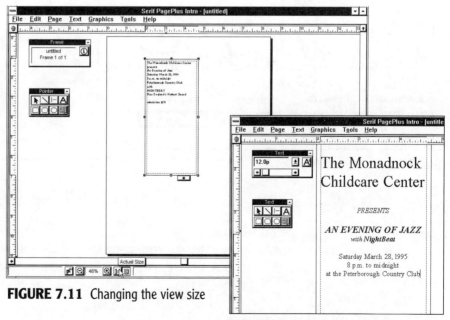

FIGURE 7.11 Changing the view size

FIGURE 7.12 Text sized for editing

Placing a Graphic

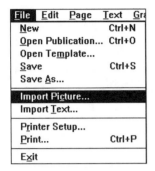

FIGURE 7.13
Importing a graphic

1. With the Text tool, pull down the File menu and click on Import Picture. See Figure 7.13.

> **→ HINT**
> When you import a graphic, it will be sized to fit the box you place it in. Adjust the box to fit your graphic or resize the graphic once it is placed.

2. The Picture Assistant window will pop up, and you can click on Art & Borders to access the clip art that comes with PagePlus. See Figure 7.14.

3. Go to the appropriate category within Art & Borders and select the clip art you want. Here we've chosen `ballroom.wmf` under the People category. See Figure 7.15.

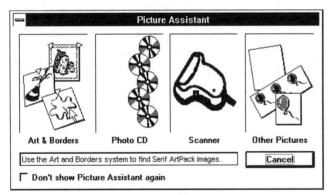

FIGURE 7.14 Accessing clip art

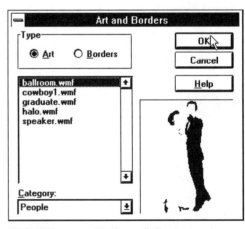

FIGURE 7.15 "Ballroom" clip art preview

4. The cursor turns into the OLE tool, which lets you create a box on the page for the graphic. The box will not show, but clicking on it will let you grab one of its handles to move or resize it. See Figure 7.16.

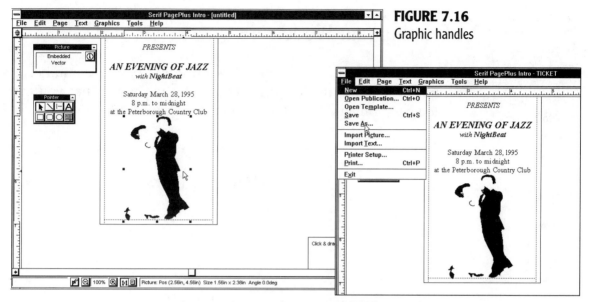

FIGURE 7.16
Graphic handles

FIGURE 7.17 Saving your ticket

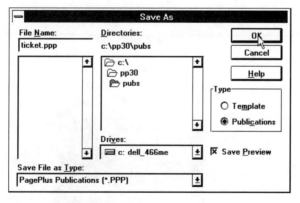

FIGURE 7.18
Creating a file name

Saving Your Work

1. Pull down the File menu and click on Save As. See Figure 7.17.

2. Give the ticket a unique name that you'll easily remember. Here we've named it **Ticket.ppp** and elected to have it stored in the Publications subdirectory (**pubs**). See Figure 7.18.

→ **PagePlus TIP**

To export your publications to different file formats, such as TIFF, BMP, or PCX files, you have to be in the Professional level of PagePlus.

→ **HINT**

If you need one end of the ticket perforated, insert a dotted line where you want the perforation. When you take the file to the printer, print out a draft copy and ask them to make a perforation on the dotted line.

Printing Your Work

Pull down the File menu and click on Print. Type the number of copies you want, in the Print dialog. Also remember that you can choose to print at different resolutions. See Figure 7.19.

FIGURE 7.19 Your finished ticket

Create Letterhead

Letterhead presents an image. Its design can range from simple to complex, with many variations in between. PagePlus comes with four templates for letterhead, each of which offers a different design. This is a perfect time to learn to create a publication from a template. Using a template enables you to use a preexisting design, replacing the objects already in place with your own objects. You can use a logo of your own design, or you can use one that's supplied with PagePlus or another software package. The letterhead we'll create in this chapter is done entirely at the Intro level.

→ PagePlus TIP
Click on the yellow lightbulb on the screen to get the PagePlus PageHint on how to use the template. (See Figure 8.2.)

Opening a Template

1. Click on File in the menu bar and choose Open Template.

2. Choose the Corporate ID category and select a letterhead template. PagePlus letterhead templates all begin with **ltrhd**. Here we've selected number 4. See Figure 8.1.

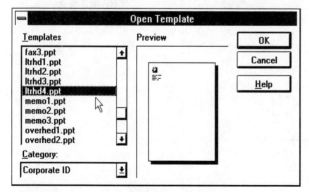

FIGURE 8.1 Choosing a template

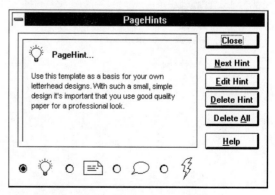

FIGURE 8.2 A PageHint on templates

HINT

Letterhead standards place company names centered or right- or left-justified at the top of the page, followed by the address, phone, fax number, and e-mail address (if appropriate).

Customizing the Letterhead

1. To see what you're doing, click on the 1:1 button to bring the text and graphics up to full size. See Figure 8.3.

2. To change the text, click on the Text tool in the tool box and type over the text that is there, or drag the mouse cursor over the text to select it, and then delete it. In Figure 8.4 we've typed over the text.

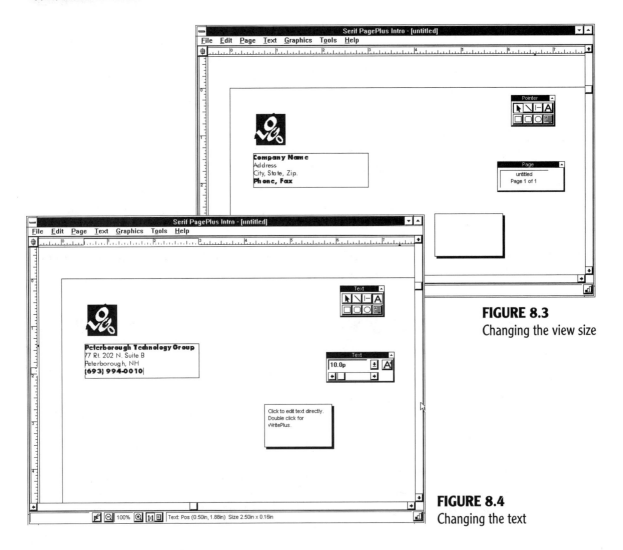

FIGURE 8.3
Changing the view size

FIGURE 8.4
Changing the text

3. To change the graphic, select the Pointer tool and click on the logo in the template. See Figure 8.5.

4. Click on File in the menu bar and select Import Picture.

5. When the Picture Assistant window pops up, select Art & Borders to pick an image to place in the logo spot. See Figure 8.6.

6. When asked whether you want to replace the selected picture or create a new one, choose Replace. See Figure 8.7.

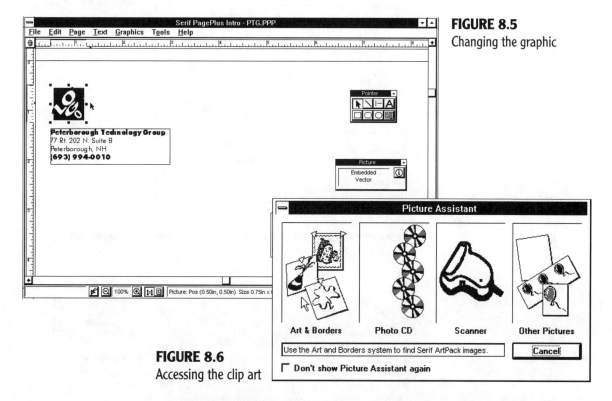

FIGURE 8.5
Changing the graphic

FIGURE 8.6
Accessing the clip art

FIGURE 8.7
Replacing your logo

7. Now select a category and whatever picture you want to use. When you select them, you can see the preview on-screen before you click OK. In Figure 8.8 we've selected `pen.wmf` from the icon category.

8. When you click OK, the selected clip art replaces the logo on the letterhead. See Figure 8.9.

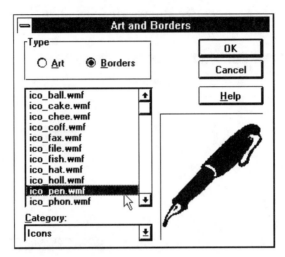

FIGURE 8.8
Choosing a new logo

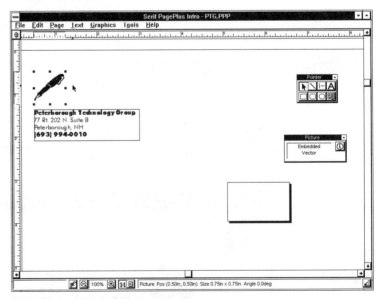

FIGURE 8.9 Your new logo in place

HINT
Design matching envelopes using the same logo, company name, and address.

9. Instant letterhead! See Figure 8.10. You're done—unless of course, you want to make further changes. If you want to move any object, just click on it and drag it to another location. You can also resize the objects.

10. Save your work! Pull down the File menu and click on Save As. Then type a unique file name and choose a subdirectory to store it in.

11. Print your letterhead. Pull down the File menu and click on Print. Print a draft copy to take to the printer, or print a few copies for your own use. (See Chapters 6 and 7 for steps on how to print PagePlus files.)

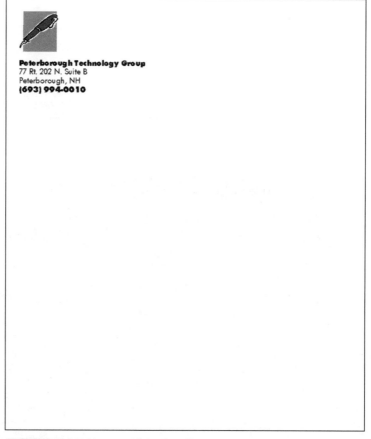

FIGURE 8.10 Your new letterhead!

Create Forms

Just about everything we do these days requires a form. If you want to make handy forms yourself, it's a snap to do with PagePlus. Before we create our own forms, however, let's take a look at the forms provided with PagePlus.

Using a Form Template

PagePlus comes with thirteen template forms, for everything from address labels to award certificates, fax cover sheets, and resumes. You can open any of these templates and modify the forms in the same manner as we did for the letterhead in Chapter 8, or roll your own.

Rolling Your Own

Forms are made up primarily of text and lines. In the previous chapters, you've learned how to add both free text and text in frames. In this chapter we'll learn to use the 45-Degree Line tool. We will only be drawing straight lines, but as simple as that sounds, it does take some practice.

1. From the StartUp Assistant window, click on Blank Page.

2. Pull down the Page menu and click on Display, then turn on Rulers, Guides, and Frames (Figure 9.1). We'll insert frames just as a guide to use for drawing the lines you need for your form.

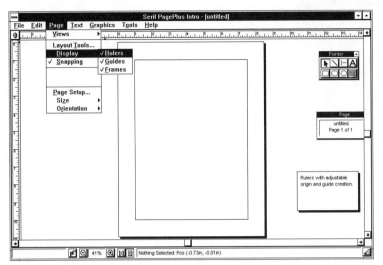

FIGURE 9.1 Turning on Rulers, Guides, and Frames

3. Select the Frame tool from the tool box and drag a frame on the page. Here we've used the ruler at the top and sides of the page to set the frame size at 7½ by 1½ inches. When you're done, the Frame Assistant window will pop up.

4. For this form, we want just a single-column text frame. Pull down the Page menu, click on Frame, and make sure that 1 is selected. See Figure 9.2.

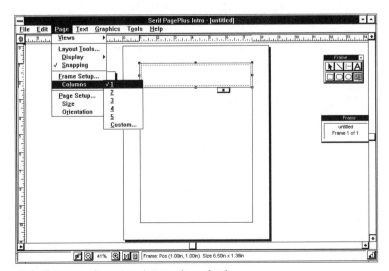

FIGURE 9.2 Choosing the number of columns

5. Select Add More Frames and all frames as described in the previous step.

6. Select the Text tool from the tool box and insert the text you want. See Figure 9.3.

7. Insert the 45-Degree Line tool from the tool box and insert lines where you want them. See Figure 9.4.

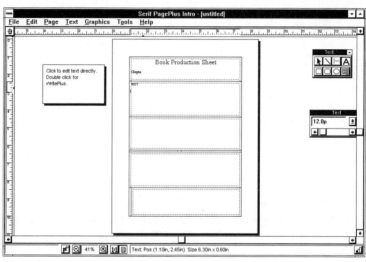

FIGURE 9.3 Entering Text

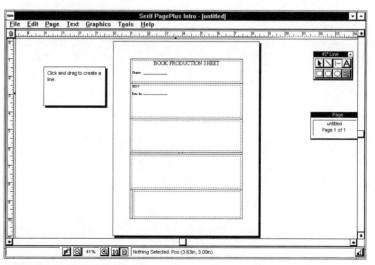

FIGURE 9.4 Creating lines

8. Continue to add elements to complete the form. See Figure 9.5.

9. Don't forget to save the file!

HINT

If you need lots of forms printed, print out a copy of your form at 300 DPI or higher, and take it to a copy shop to make multiple copies.

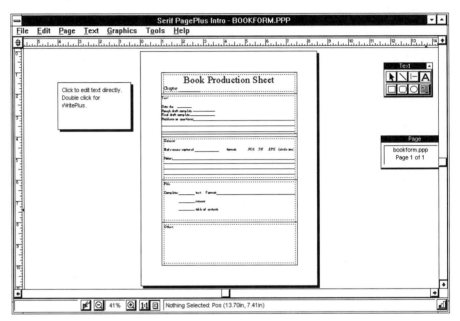

FIGURE 9.5 A complete form

Create a Poster or Sign

Creating a poster or sign involves little more than placing text and graphics on-screen, but in this chapter we'll get a bit fancy and rotate some text. To do this we'll move up a level, to Publisher. Choose PagePlus Level from the Tools pull-down menu, or click on the button in the lower-right corner of the window that displays the three levels. Then select Publisher from the list of levels.

In this chapter we'll also work with a larger page size, and we'll learn how to select different fonts.

PagePlus allows you to go up to a 22- by 22-inch page, which is large enough for most uses. To get a page that large, you have to set it by pulling down the Page menu, clicking on Size, and then on Custom. Standard page sizes are:

Letter	(8.5" by 11")
Legal	(8.5" by 14")
Tabloid	(11" by 17")
A3	(11.69" by 16.53")
A4	(8.27" by 11.69")
A5	(5.85" by 8.27")
B5	(6.93" by 9.84")

> **→ HINT**
>
> Make sure that your printer can handle whatever page size you want to print. Otherwise, take the file to a commercial printer, where you can have it printed on poster stock.

Setting Up the Page

1. Choose Blank Page from the StartUp Assistant window.

2. You can select the page size in one of two ways. Pull down the Page menu, click on Size, and select the size you want. Or, pull down the Page menu, click on Size, then click on Custom, and scroll through the standard page sizes or create your own. In Figure 10.1 we'll select Tabloid from the list.

FIGURE 10.1
Choosing a page size

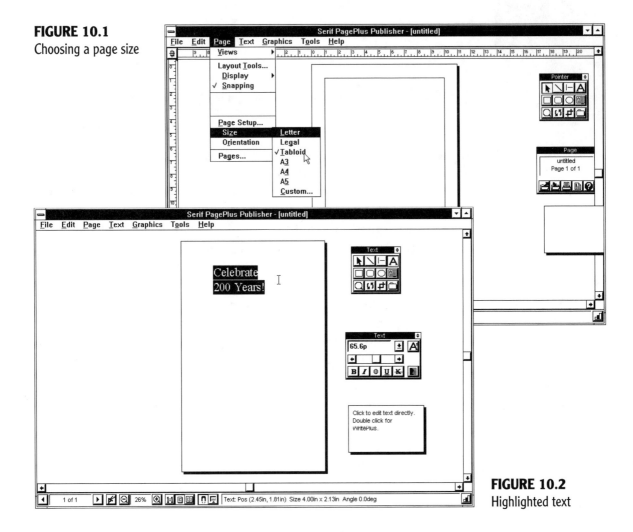

FIGURE 10.2
Highlighted text

Placing and Rotating Text

1. Select the Text tool from the tool box and place some text on the page as shown in Figure 10.2. Increase the size of the text using the slider on the change bar.

2. To rotate the text, select the Pointer tool from the tool box and click anywhere on the text. The text should be surrounded by eight small black handles, as shown in Figure 10.3, indicating that the text is now selected.

→ PagePlus TIP

To rotate an object in 45-degree increments, hold down the SHIFT key after you start the rotation. When you're satisfied with the position, let go of the mouse and then release the SHIFT key.

3. Select the rotate tool from the tool box. Grab the top left handle and rotate the text to a position you're satisfied with. See Figure 10.4.

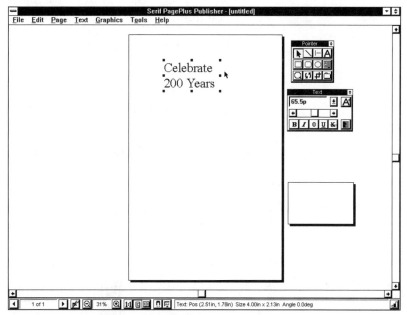

FIGURE 10.3 Select text with handles

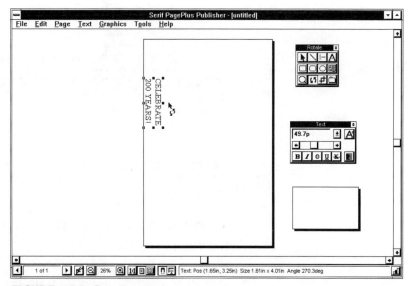

FIGURE 10.4 Rotating text

Placing a Graphic

1. Select the Pointer tool from the tool box and pull down the File menu.

2. Click on Import Picture and select a picture from the dialog that pops up.

3. The cursor turns into an OLE tool. Draw a box using that tool, and click to insert the picture. See Figure 10.5.

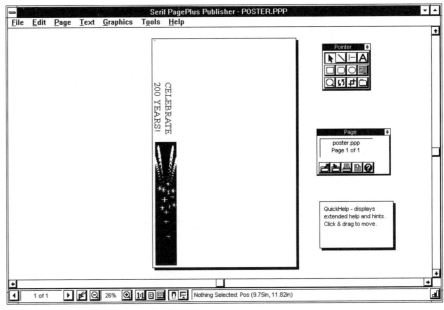

FIGURE 10.5 The graphic in place

Changing Fonts

1. Select the Text tool from the tool box and select the text you want to change.

2. Click on the Property Palette button on the change bar and select the Font tool. See Figure 10.6.

→ **PagePlus TIP**

As you change fonts, the size of the type may change. Resize the type using the property palette and the Size button. Use the slider or the arrow keys on the change bar to change the type size.

3. Move the slider or the arrows on the change bar and watch the font of the selected text change. Stop when you find a font that you like. See Figure 10.7.

FIGURE 10.6 Selecting the Font tool on the property palette

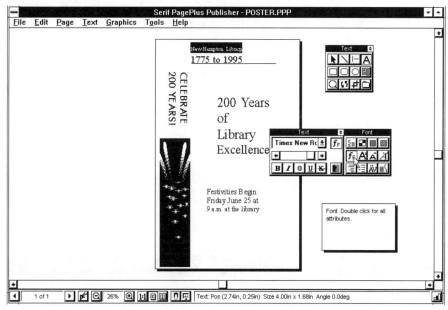

FIGURE 10.7
Changing the type size with the change bar slider

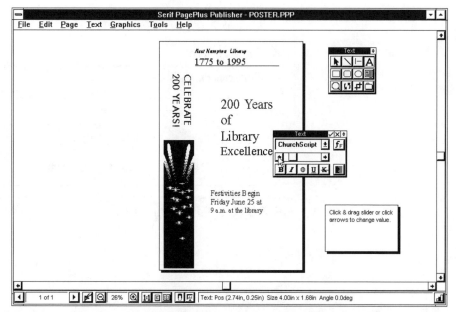

Printing the Poster

1. Print your poster on your own printer if it has the capability to print the page size you've created. After saving the poster one last time, pull down the File menu and choose Print. To change the paper size, choose Setup and select a paper size from the dialog. See Figure 10.8.

2. To export the poster as a file, switch to the Professional level. Select Export as Picture from the File pull-down menu and click the appropriate settings in the dialog. See Figure 10.9.

3. Take the file to a commercial printer or service bureau to be printed on poster stock. You can also get the poster laminated or mounted. Ask your printer what your options are. See Chapter 16 for more information on working with a commercial printer or service bureau.

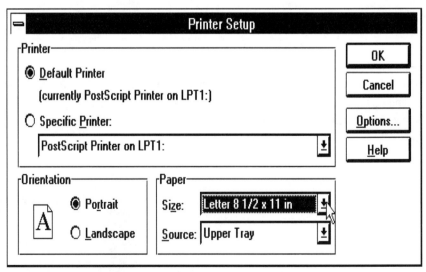

FIGURE 10.8 Printer setup dialog

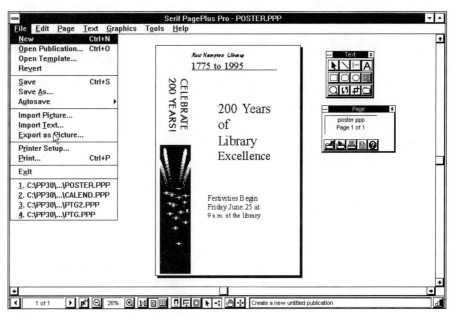

FIGURE 10.9 Exporting your poster

Create a One-Page Press Release

Designing a press release demands more communications ability than creativity. First you must know who your audience is and what the release must convey to that audience. Be sure to give the appropriate contact information. The design is also important, because the better your message looks, the better you communicate that message.

In this chapter we'll work at the Publisher level to create a very simple news release. You already know many of the basics from previous chapters, but we'll go one step further and import both a graphic and text from an outside source. In this case we'll use a company logo that has been stored as an EPS (encapsulated PostScript) file, which we'll pull in from a floppy disk. The text is stored as a Microsoft Word file, which we'll also pull in from a floppy disk. This is a real-life example because, in many cases, the art you use comes from a designer and the text from a writer. Whether you take your text and graphics from a floppy disk, a hard drive, or a network doesn't really matter. The lesson here is on importing a file from any type of outside source.

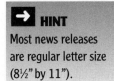

HINT
Most news releases are regular letter size (8½" by 11").

Setting Up the Page

1. Choose Blank Page from the StartUp Assistant window.

2. Make sure Snapping is turned on and Rulers, Guides, and Frames are displayed. Do this by pulling down the Page menu and clicking on Display, as shown in Figure 11.1.

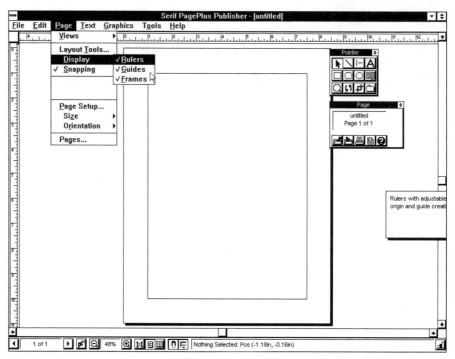

FIGURE 11.1 Getting ready

Importing a Graphic

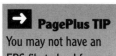

1. Insert the company logo by selecting the Pointer tool and clicking on Import Picture in the File menu.

2. When the Picture Assistant window pops up, click on Other Pictures. See Figure 11.2.

3. Make sure the floppy disk containing the logo is in the drive. Then, in the Import Picture dialog, select the proper drive. Also select what type of file you want to import. Under File Name in the dialog, you should get a list of all the files on the disk with the extension you specify. For example, Figure 11.3 shows all .EPS files on drive A:. When you click on the file name you want, you'll see a picture of it in the preview box on the right side of the dialog.

FIGURE 11.2
Accessing outside pictures

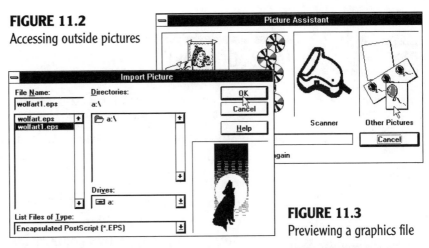

FIGURE 11.3
Previewing a graphics file

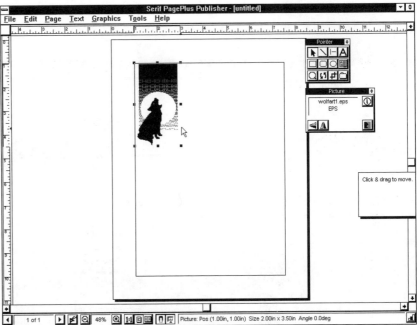

FIGURE 11.4 Positioning and sizing a graphic

4. When you click OK the cursor turns into the OLE tool (which you are probably used to working with by now). Using the OLE tool, drag the box with the graphic in it to wherever you want the logo to go. Here we'll position it in the upper left corner. Using the rules as a guide, we'll size it to 2 inches wide by 3½ inches long. You can resize it by grabbing one of the eight little square handles. See Figure 11.4.

HINT
Save your work.

Importing Text

1. To insert a header at the top of the page, click on the Type tool and type in the text you want. Adjust the size and font using the change bar palettes. In Figure 11.5 we've chosen Technical for the typeface, and it's set at 39.9 points.

2. Now it's time to import the text. Select the Frame tool and drag out a frame, as shown. When the Frame Assistant window pops up, click Cancel to tell it to go away. PagePlus assumes you want a two-column text frame, but in this case we just want one. To change this, click on the single-column frame shown in the change bar, Figure 11.6.

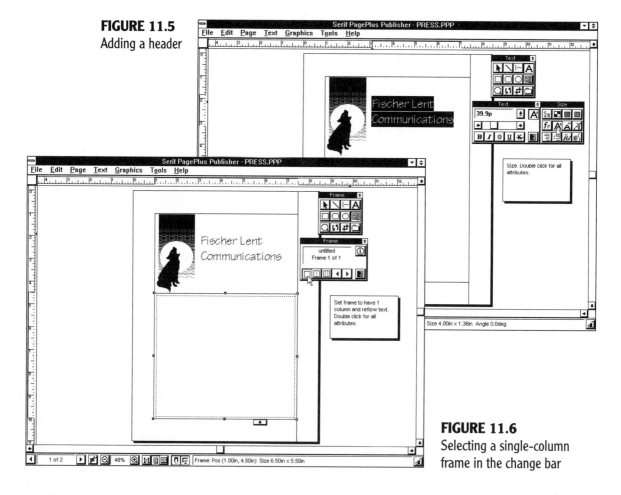

FIGURE 11.5
Adding a header

FIGURE 11.6
Selecting a single-column frame in the change bar

3. To import text, click on the Text tool. Go to the File pull-down menu and click on Import Text.

4. The Import Text dialog pops up (Figure 11.7). Click on the drive letter where the text is stored. In this case it's drive A:. Then select the type of document; here it's a Microsoft Word file. Type in the file name. The boxes labeled Retain Format and Ignore Returns are important here. We'll check to Retain Format, which will import text just as it appears on the incoming file. Ignore Returns will do away with carriage returns, which is something we don't want to do in this case.

5. The text will flow into the text frame, beginning wherever you position the mouse pointer. See Figure 11.9.

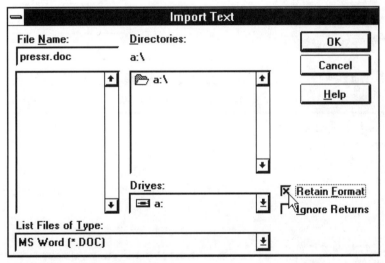

FIGURE 11.7 The Import Text dialog

 HINT
OOPS! Don't forget to insert the correct disk into the drive, or you'll get the error message shown in Figure 11.8.

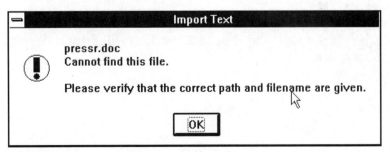

FIGURE 11.8 Wrong disk!

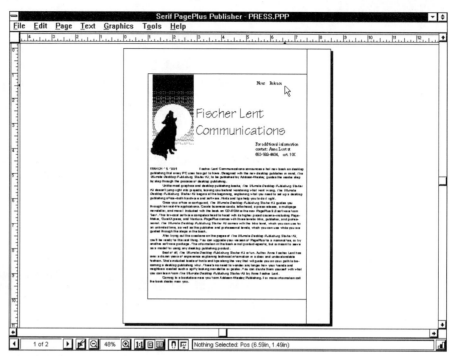

FIGURE 11.9 Imported text

➡ **HINT**

Use high-quality paper. Companies such as Paper Direct specialize in desktop publishing papers that are perfect for adding color and pizzazz to what would otherwise be a plain black-and-white news release.

6. Add whatever finishing touches you want. For example, before outputting the final version, we'll add contact information and adjust the position of the header.

➡ **HINT**

For reliable printing, make sure you have the latest Windows printer driver. The current PostScript driver is `pscript.drv` v3.58.

Printing the Press Release

After saving the news release one last time, pull down the File menu and choose Print. This will print it on your desktop printer.

12

Create a Greeting Card

Many occasions call for a greeting card. With your increasing desktop publishing ability, it'll be easier than ever to create your own. The card we'll create is a Season's Greeting card with a business look, but you can use the same model to create a birth announcement with a photo, a birthday card, or any other type of card you can imagine. Print just one or thousands.

The card designed here is done at the Publisher level. We'll add a border to the card from the PagePlus Arts & Borders collection. The card is a standard 6- by 4½-inch size, which will fit in a standard A6 envelope. You can choose to make cards in whatever size you like.

Setting Up the Page

1. Choose Blank Page from the StartUp Assistant window.

2. From the Page menu, scroll down to Page Setup and choose Orientation. Click on Wide (which is the same as landscape). See Figure 12.1.

3. To create a 6- by 4½-inch card, you need to create a 6- by 9-inch page, which is then folded in half. To create a 6- by 9-inch page, pull down the Page menu, click on Size, and choose Custom. See Figure 12.2.

4. When the Page Setup dialog pops up, set Width at 9.00 and Height at 6.00. See Figure 12.3.

5. Before positioning text or borders on the page, we need to create frames that accommodate a margin on each side of the card, including at the center, where the card will be folded. We can set the top and side margins within the Page Setup

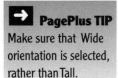

PagePlus TIP
Make sure that Wide orientation is selected, rather than Tall.

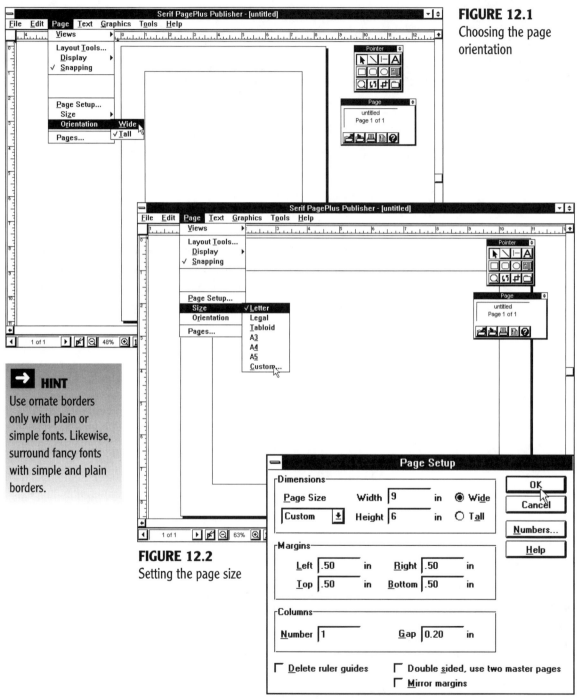

FIGURE 12.1
Choosing the page orientation

→ HINT
Use ornate borders only with plain or simple fonts. Likewise, surround fancy fonts with simple and plain borders.

FIGURE 12.2
Setting the page size

FIGURE 12.3 The Page Setup dialog

→ PagePlus TIP
To move the tool box and change bar, click on the blue bar along the top of each and, holding the mouse button down, slide the box to wherever you want it. We'll move it to the left so we can see the right side of the page.

dialog. As shown in Figure 12.3, we've set each margin, Left, Right, Top, and Bottom, to .50 inches.

6. Now select the Frame tool and drag out a frame on the left side, starting at the guide that designates the left margin and dragging over to the 4-inch mark on the ruler. Then drag it down to the bottom guide. This gives you a frame of 3½ by 5 inches, which is just right for a ½-inch border on all sides of a 6- by 4½-inch card. See Figure 12.4.

7. To create the frame on the right side, repeat the process; only this time, start at the 5-inch mark on the ruler and drag the frame over to the guide that marks the margin on the right, and then down to the guide on the bottom. See Figure 12.5.

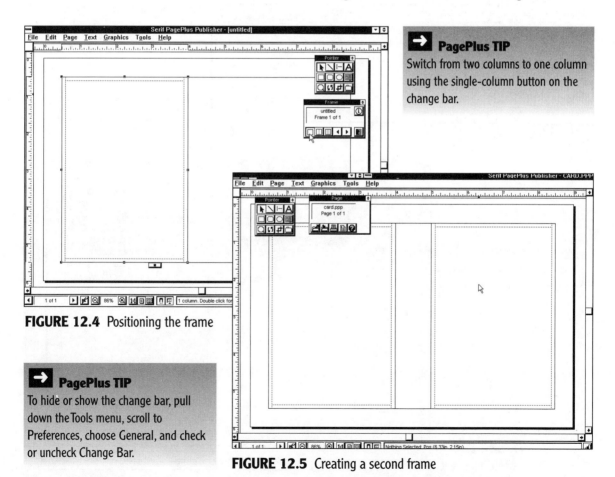

FIGURE 12.4 Positioning the frame

FIGURE 12.5 Creating a second frame

→ PagePlus TIP
Switch from two columns to one column using the single-column button on the change bar.

→ PagePlus TIP
To hide or show the change bar, pull down the Tools menu, scroll to Preferences, choose General, and check or uncheck Change Bar.

Positioning Text

1. The text you enter on the left side will appear on the back of the card. This can be used to add a professional or humorous touch to your card (depending of course on what you write). Enter some text as shown in Figure 12.6.

2. Align the text by selecting it with the Text tool, pulling down the Text menu, choosing Align, and clicking on Left. See Figure 12.7.

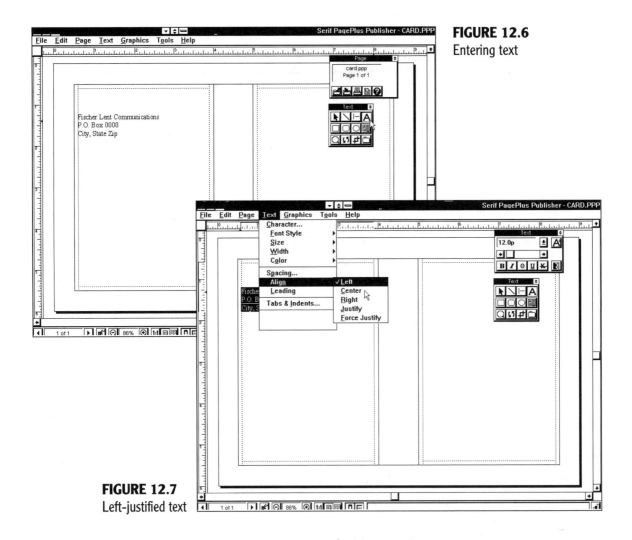

FIGURE 12.6
Entering text

FIGURE 12.7
Left-justified text

→ **PagePlus TIP**
Move the text down by placing the cursor in front of the text and pressing Return on your keyboard until the text is positioned where you want it.

3. To choose a font, select the text with the Text tool and click on the "A" button on the change bar to display the flyout. Click on the Font button and select a font from the change bar. Here we'll select Technical. See Figure 12.8.

4. To change the size, repeat Step 3, but click on the Size button and select the size with the change bar slider or arrows. See Figure 12.9.

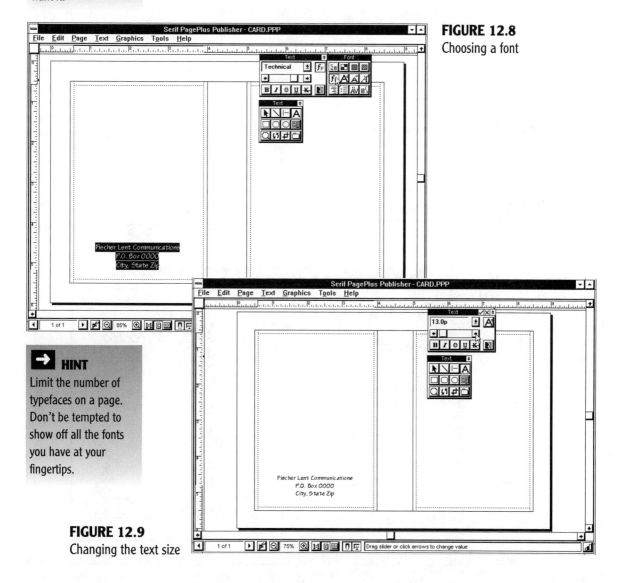

FIGURE 12.8
Choosing a font

→ **HINT**
Limit the number of typefaces on a page. Don't be tempted to show off all the fonts you have at your fingertips.

FIGURE 12.9
Changing the text size

Adding a Decorative Border

1. To add a border to the front of the card, pull down the File menu and click on Import Picture.

2. When the Picture Assistant window pops up, select Arts & Borders.

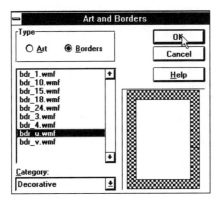

FIGURE 12.10 Choosing the border

3. Scroll through the borders listed and select the one you want. In Figure 12.10 we've selected a red and white checked border, for that holiday look.

4. The cursor will turn into the placement tool. Just press the left mouse button and hold it down while you drag the tool across the page and down. Let go of the button, and voila! You have a border. See Figure 12.11.

FIGURE 12.11
Adding the border

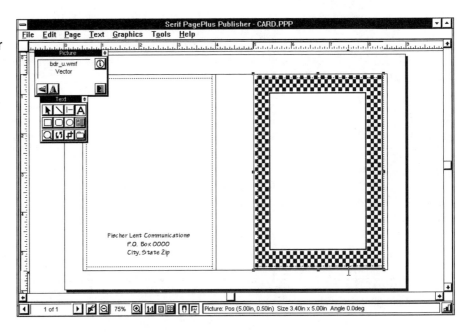

Adding a Page

1. To print the front and back of the card, we have to print two pages. The simplest way to add a second page is to click on the arrow button at the bottom of the PagePlus window, to the right of the status bar that reads "1 of 1." See Figure 12.12.

2. A box pops up labeled Pages (Figure 12.13). Make sure Add blank page(s) is selected and that you are adding 1 blank page at page 2. Then click OK.

3. Following the procedure described in Step 6 under "Setting up the Page," drag out a frame on the right side of the page that measures 3½ inches across by 5 inches high. See Figure 12.14.

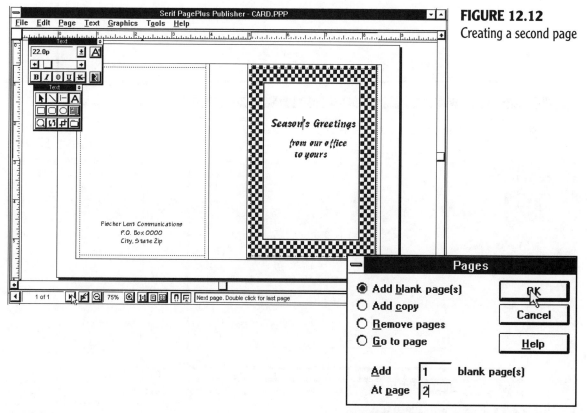

FIGURE 12.12
Creating a second page

FIGURE 12.13 Adding blank pages

4. Add text, following the method described under "Positioning Text." See Figure 12.15.

5. Add any final touches you may want, such as a photo or a company logo, using Import Picture under the File menu.

PagePlus TIP

If you want to go back to page 1, press the left arrow button on the bottom of the screen, which is to the left of the button that says "2 of 2."

FIGURE 12.14
Adding a frame

FIGURE 12.15 Page 2 with added text

Printing the Greeting Card

You can print out a sample of your card on your own desktop printer using regular paper, or try a heavier stock (80 lb. is recommended) if you need to print just a few. To do this, you have to print one page, then turn the paper over and print the second page on the other side.

1. Pull down the File menu and click Print. Select Setup from the Print dialog, click on Landscape mode, and then click OK. See Figure 12.16.

2. Back in the Print dialog, under Print Range, choose Pages and type in the number 1 in both the From and To boxes, as shown here. This will print just the first page. See Figure 12.17.

3. After you've printed the first page, repeat the printing procedure for page 2. But first take the sheet you printed page 1 on and turn it over so you can print on the other side. When it comes out of the printer the second time, fold it, and you have a card.

PagePlus TIP

If you saved your work in color and plan to have the card printed in color, click on Color Separate in the Print dialog box.

HINT

To print a quantity of cards, print out a sample as described and take it, along with the file on a floppy disk, to a commercial printer. Printing on 80 lb. uncoated cover stock will give you a professional-looking card. Commercial printers can fold the cards for you automatically.

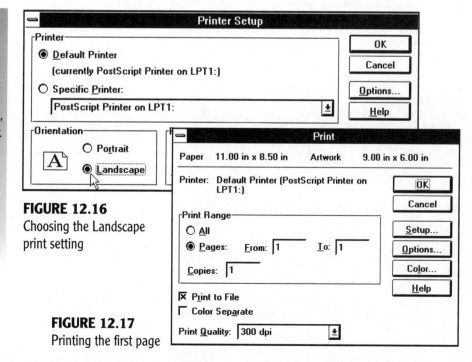

FIGURE 12.16
Choosing the Landscape print setting

FIGURE 12.17
Printing the first page

Create a Brochure

Promoting yourself, your business, or your products has never been simpler. By creating a two-sided brochure, you can convey loads of information for the cost of a single postage stamp. The brochure we'll create here doesn't even need an envelope. Side two will include your return address and a space for a mailing label.

This is the last project we'll create at the Publisher level. This lesson covers how to use a template, import text and graphics, and select and change colors. Coloring objects is the only part of the lesson that we have not touched on in previous chapters. However, you don't have to produce a brochure in color. And some people opt to print the text and graphics in black, but to use a colored stock. Color does, however, add a touch of class to your promotion. All it takes is a few clicks of the mouse button in PagePlus and other desktop publishing programs to switch from basic black and white to the sophistication of a four-color publication

 HINT
Brochures promote a product or service, lure customers, or sell specific items.

Selecting a Template

1. When you first start up PagePlus, choose Templates in the StartUp Assistant window.

2. PagePlus organizes its templates into several categories. Scroll down to Sales & Promotion and click on OK.

3. In the list of templates available under that topic, scroll down to `broch2.ppt`. Click on OK, as shown in Figure 13.1.

4. Up pops the template, complete with text and graphics (Figure 13.2).

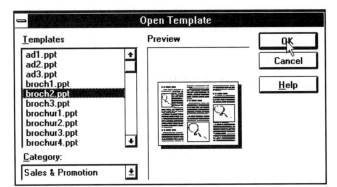

FIGURE 13.1
Choosing a template

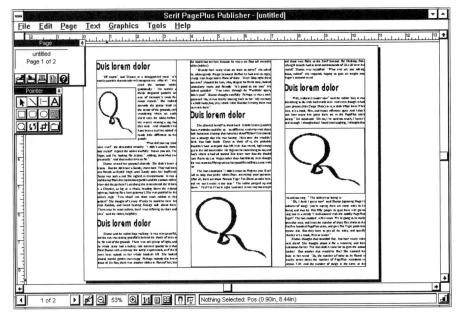

FIGURE 13.2 The broch2 template

➡ **PagePlus TIP**
You can import text
from a variety of word
processors. Make sure
that PagePlus supports
the format you want to
import by pulling down
the File menu, clicking
Import Text, and check-
ing the formats listed
under "List Files of
Type."

Importing Text

The text we've imported here is about four hundred words in length
and was written in Microsoft Word. The text is formatted, which
means that a font was selected in Word and the text was sized. The
subheads are set in bold type.

➜ PagePlus TIP
If the import text is too long for the template, it will automatically flow onto page 2. You can adjust it to fit after the text has flowed.

1. To import text, select the Text tool from the tool box and select the text at the top of the template.

2. Pull down the File menu, scroll down to Import Text, and click on OK. When the following dialog pops up, click on Replace. See Figure 13.3.

3. The Import Text dialog will pop up (Figure 13.4). In this box, select the file you want to import. Also select Retain Format, so the font and text size you've set in your document will be retained. Don't select Ignore Returns, or you'll lose your paragraph formatting.

4. When you click OK in the Import Text dialog, your import text automatically flows onto the template. See Figure 13.5.

5. Make whatever adjustments are necessary to the text at this time. Try changing the size of subheads, adding bold or italic to elements you want to stand out, and so on. Also take a look at the white space, and adjust it accordingly.

FIGURE 13.3
Replacing text in a template

➜ PagePlus TIP
When you make a change, if it appears not to have taken effect or if the type overwrites type that's already there, pull down the File menu and click on Save. This will reflow the page and should straighten out anything that appears to be an error.

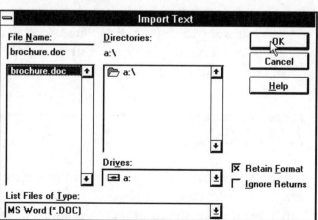

FIGURE 13.4
The Import Text dialog

HINT

A brochure printed on an 8½" by 11" stock, folded in thirds, will fit in a standard business-size envelope.

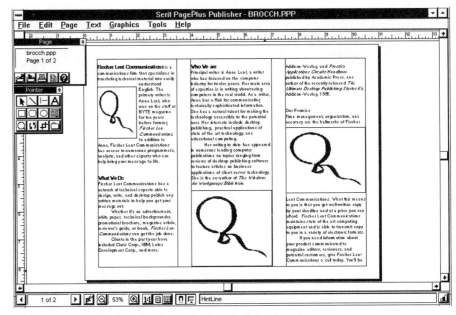

FIGURE 13.5 The imported text displayed on the template

Importing Graphics

 HINT

In this brochure, the graphics came from an EPS file stored on the hard drive, as well as from Serif's ArtPack collection of clip art. You can import graphics from many sources, including Photo CDs. See Chapter 16 for more information on importing images.

1. To replace the graphics on the template, select them one at a time using the Pointer tool.

2. Import graphics in the same way as we did for the press release in Chapter 11. When you select the type of graphic you want to import, PagePlus asks if you want to replace the selected picture or create a new one. Click Replace, as we did when importing text. See Figure 13.6.

Adding Color

PagePlus lets you add spot color and process color to both text and graphics. Spot color consists of solid color; process color, on the other hand, is made up of a combination of cyan, magenta, yellow,

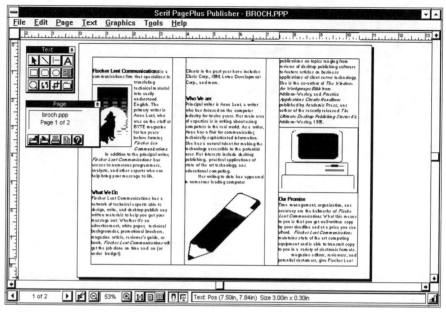

FIGURE 13.6 Imported graphics

and black. For our brochure we'll change the border around each graphic to a color, as well as add color to the subheads and leading text. Since we're adding a minimal amount of color, spot color will be sufficient. For process color, which requires color separations, you should have a professional printer or service bureau do your printing. But for spot color, your color desktop printer will most likely meet your needs.

Adding color to objects in PagePlus is as easy as moving the slider on the change bar.

1. Select the object you want to color. If it's text, use the Text tool. If it's a graphic, use the Pointer tool.

2. Click on the "A" in the change bar to show the flyout. Then click on the box with the four colors in it. See Figure 13.7.

3. Use the slider on the change bar as you would to change any property of an object. To change the color, slide the slider. You'll see the color of the selected object change immediately. See Figure 13.8.

**PagePlus TIP**

If you want to "edit" the PagePlus colors, pull down the Graphics menu and click on Color. Then click on Palette, and the Edit Colors dialog pops up.

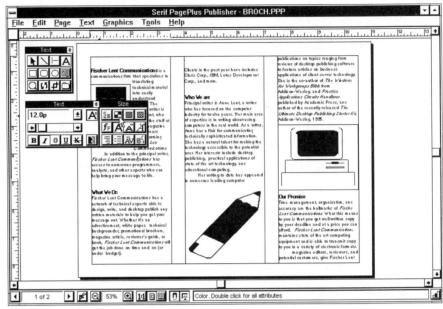

FIGURE 13.7 The Color button on the change bar flyout

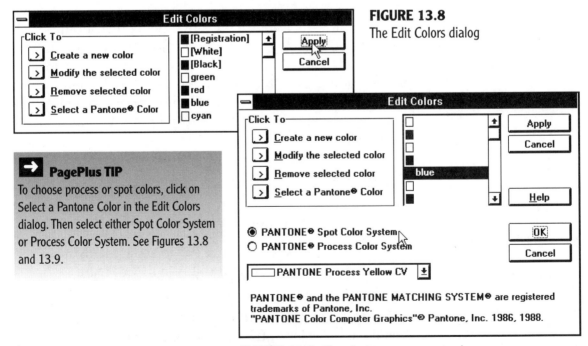

FIGURE 13.8
The Edit Colors dialog

**PagePlus TIP**

To choose process or spot colors, click on Select a Pantone Color in the Edit Colors dialog. Then select either Spot Color System or Process Color System. See Figures 13.8 and 13.9.

FIGURE 13.9 Choosing process or spot color

Page Two

1. Click on the right arrow at the bottom left of the screen (next to where it says "1 of 2").

2. In the far right column of page 2, select the text you want to change and type in new text.

3. To change the address label text and return address, double-click on them. This will call up WritePlus. Type your new text over the old text in WritePlus and click on the check mark in the lower right corner to accept the changes. Your new text will automatically replace the old text on the brochure. See Figure 13.10.

4. Insert your logo where it says "logo" on the template, or delete "logo," as I did on the brochure shown here. (To insert a logo, use the same method used previously for inserting graphics. To delete it, select "logo" and press Delete.) See Figure 13.11.

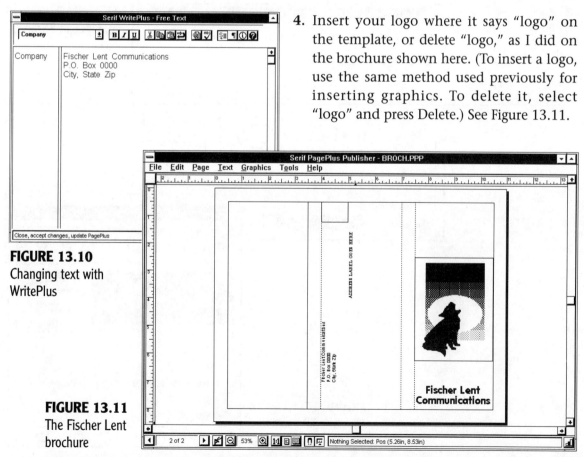

FIGURE 13.10
Changing text with WritePlus

FIGURE 13.11
The Fischer Lent brochure

Color Separation

1. To separate colors, pull down the Print menu and click on Color Separate. See Figure 13.12.

2. To separate process colors, click on Process in the Color Separation dialog. When you print your document, you will get four sheets for each page—one for each color (cyan, magenta, yellow, and black). See Figure 13.13.

3. To "separate" spot colors, click Spot in the Color Separations dialog. When you print, you will get one sheet for each color used on each page. See Figure 13.14.

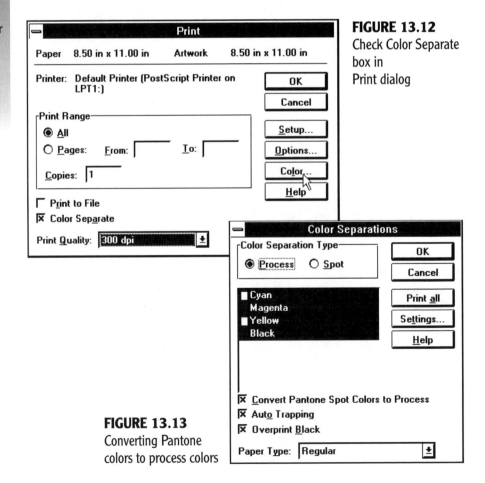

FIGURE 13.12
Check Color Separate box in
Print dialog

FIGURE 13.13
Converting Pantone
colors to process colors

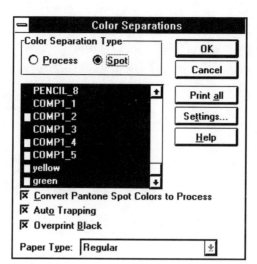

FIGURE 13.14
Separating spot colors

Printing the Brochure

To print your brochure on a desktop printer, use the same method described in Chapter 12 for printing a greeting card: first print one page, then take the paper out of the printer, turn it over, and print the second page.

For professional-looking results, take your brochure to a printer or service bureau. Print one master copy as in Chapter 12 and take it, along with a disk with the color separation files, to the printer. A 65 pound uncoated cover stock will hold up well in the mail and will give you the professional look you want.

If you use any size other than the standard 8½- by 11-inch mailer, you may want to bring it down to your local post office to find out if it meets postal regulations for mailing. You don't want to invest your time, creativity, and money on a project only to find that it can't be mailed!

Create an Advertisement

When you promote anything, first impressions count. What you say is important, but even more important is that the typeface, graphics, and general look of the page catch the reader's eye. Start with a clear message that is well written and honed specifically to your audience. Then back up that message with a layout, graphics, and type that will help broadcast the message to your readers.

The paper it's printed on is equally important, so choose carefully here, as well. If your advertisement will run in a publication, you may have to go with the paper that the rest of the publication is printed on, which in some cases is abysmal. But if you're willing to pay for it, you may be able to get your ad printed on a heavier stock, making it stand out from the rest at first glance.

This project is done at the Professional level—which doesn't mean it's more difficult, but rather that we have more tools at our fingertips. The yellow quick help box has disappeared, and a style palette and status editor have appeared, as have a few other added extras.

The style palette makes it easy to apply consistent styles to text and graphics. We've been applying styles, but we haven't been naming and saving them for future use. The style palette lets you do this with ease.

The status editor is activated by a button found on the bar along the bottom of the PagePlus window. If you want to change the position or angle of an object, you simply select the object and click on the Status Editor button. Up pops the Status Editor dialog, which lets you change the position, width, height, or rotation of the object.

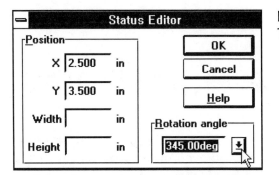

FIGURE 14.1
The Status Editor dialog

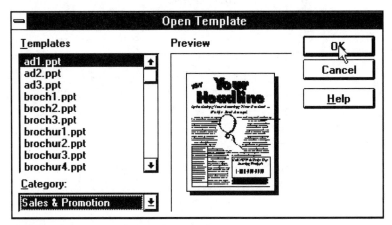

FIGURE 14.2 Selecting a template

Selecting a Template

PagePlus comes with three templates for advertisements. We'll use a template for a four-color 8½- by 11-inch ad, to which you can add your own text and graphics.

1. When you start PagePlus, click on Templates in the StartUp Assistant window.

2. In the Open Template dialog, scroll down to the Sales & Promotion category and select it.

3. Under Templates, select `ad1.ppt`, as shown in Figure 14.2.

4. Click OK and the template opens on the screen before you. See Figure 14.3.

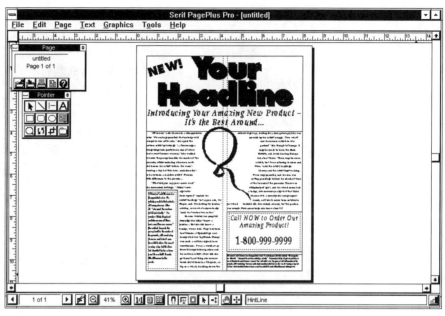

FIGURE 14.3 The `ad1.ppt` template

Importing Text

As with our previous projects, you can type in text directly, import it from a different word processor, or enter it via WritePlus. We'll do a combination of importing from a Word file and typing text directly to the template.

1. Select the headline text using the Arrow tool from the tool box. Delete the text twice, since it is in two layers. (The layers consist of two different colors, one placed over the other, to give it a layered look.) Type in your new text. Do the same with the subhead and the text in the text box below. See Figure 14.4.

→ PagePlus TIP

To get colored text with a colored outline:

• Make sure "snapping" is turned on. Pull down the Page menu and look for a check mark next to Snapping.

• Select the text you want to apply this effect to. Here we've selected the headline by using the Pointer tool in the tool box.

• Copy the text onto itself by holding down the Ctrl key while you click and hold the pointer on the object. Before you release the mouse button, move the mouse just a tiny bit.

• You now have two copies of your text. You can give them different colors by selecting them individually with the Pointer tool, choosing the Color button from the Text fly-out palette, and then moving the slider on the change bar to the desired color. Here we've chosen navy blue on top and red on the bottom. See Figure 14.5.

FIGURE 14.4 New headline text

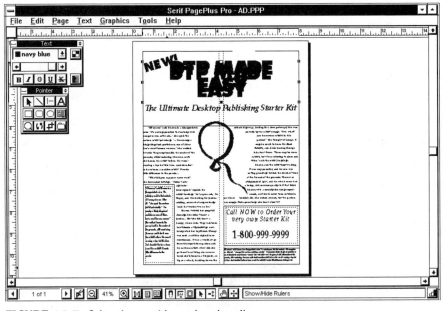

FIGURE 14.5 Colored text with a colored outline

2. To import text, highlight the text you want to replace. See Figure 14.6.

3. Pull down the File menu and click on Import Text. You'll be asked if you want to Replace, Append, or Cancel. Click on Replace, which will replace the selected text with the text you want to import. See Figure 14.7.

PagePlus TIP

If your text is too long and flows onto a second page, you can delete that second page by pulling down the Page menu and clicking on Pages. When the Pages window appears, select Remove pages and enter 2, for the beginning and ending of the range, as shown in Figure 14.8.

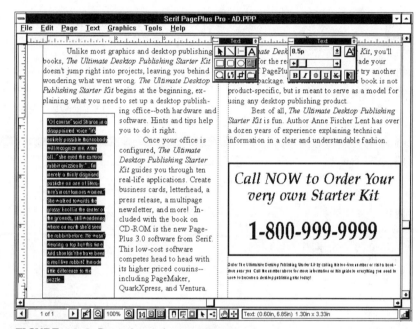

FIGURE 14.6 Preparing to import text

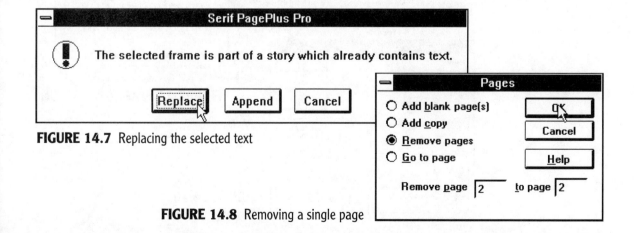

FIGURE 14.7 Replacing the selected text

FIGURE 14.8 Removing a single page

Importing Graphics and Wrapping Text

1. Replace the graphic in the template in the same way as we did in Chapter 13. Select the graphic with the Pointer tool, pull down the File menu, click on Import Picture, and choose the source file you want to import.

2. After selecting the graphic you want to import, put it in position using the OLE tool. See Figure 14.9.

3. To wrap text around the graphic, select it and then pull down the Tools menu and click on Wrap Settings. In the Wrap Settings dialog, click on Wrap Outside, as shown in Figure 14.10.

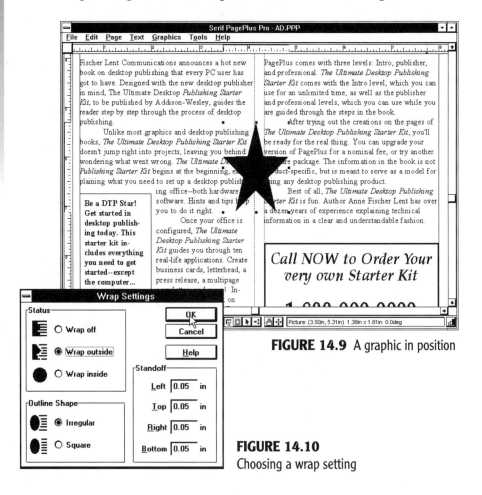

FIGURE 14.9 A graphic in position

FIGURE 14.10
Choosing a wrap setting

Creating or Changing Styles

Anything you create in PagePlus has styles applied to it, whether you apply them consciously or not. As you become a more sophisticated desktop publisher, it will become more important to you to preserve some of the styles you've created. Saving the styles you use in your publications lets you give a consistent look to everything you produce. It's also quicker to just click on a named style than to scroll through several formatting commands to adjust the font, type size, alignment, and more. You can always change styles or add new ones. Follow these simple steps:

1. Once you've decided that you like a style you see on-screen, save it by pulling down the Text menu, clicking on Text Style, and then on Palette. See Figure 14.11.

2. When the Text Style palette pops up, click on Save Styles as Style Sheet. See Figure 14.12.

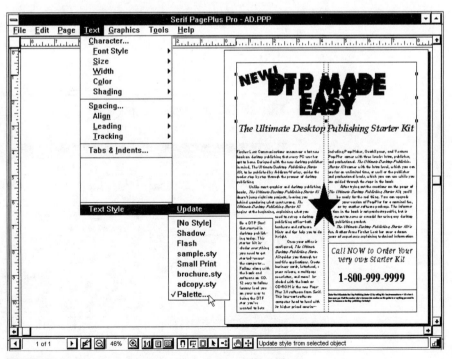

FIGURE 14.11 Saving a style

3. To modify a style, select the style you want to change, click on Palette, and choose Modify the Selected Style.

4. Then, in the box at the botom of the dialog, choose Character Attributes, Spacing and Alignment, or Tabs and Indents, depending on what you want to change. If you choose Character Attributes, a window pops up showing you the character attributes currently assigned to that style. Just click on whatever you want to change, whether it's color, font, case, effect, or more.

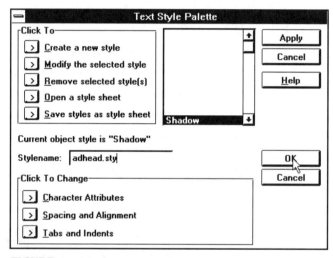

FIGURE 14.12 Creating a style sheet

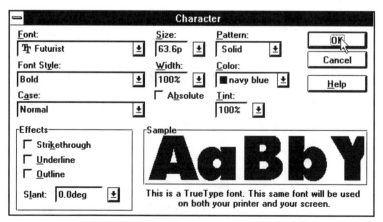

FIGURE 14.13 Naming a style

Outputting the Ad

Ideally, a four-color ad should be printed in four colors on the nicest stock available. However, as much as you may wish for control over its final printing, the reality is that you may have to adhere to the rules of the publication in which the ad will run. For example, your local newspaper may only print in black and white and may work only from camera-ready art. A slick four-color trade journal may only print four-color advertisements, and might expect film rather than camera-ready art. Knowing where and how your ad will be reproduced is critical for getting the best results. Check with the publication that will be running your ad to find out what they need. Then talk to your professional printer or service bureau to find out what they need to get the job done to your specifications.

Create a Multipage Newsletter

Newsletters are everywhere. We all receive loads of them in the mail. Some we read and some we toss out (recycle, of course). The purpose of a newsletter is to convey specific information to a targeted audience. Most newsletters come out on a fairly regular basis, whether monthly, bimonthly, quarterly, or whatever. Before designing your newsletter, you must be able to define the purpose for your newsletter and who the readers are.

The technology of desktop publishing makes newsletter production very easy—this may be why we see so many newsletters today. But you don't want to run the risk of being just another publication that passes from the mailbox to the recycling bin. What can set your creation apart is the thought you put into it. Choose a format that will work for you now and in the future. Don't make it too complex, or you'll dread the thought of deadline day. Also, consider how to set off each section of the newsletter while maintaining a consistent look. This will not only help you in creating the newsletter, but it will also help your readers identify the sections that are of the most interest to them. For example, if you have a calendar in your newsletter, keep its look and placement consistent.

Think of the parts of your newsletter as modules. You can mix column formats on a page—for example, place a wide-column story next to a single column. You can also mix clip art, photos, tables, charts, and other graphics on the page for a strong visual image. But, as with all desktop publishing creations, be careful not to overdo it. Pace the stories with art, to help your reader absorb all the information you'll pack into each issue. And place white space judiciously to give the eye a break.

This lesson is done at the Professional level; it incorporates a little bit of everything you've learned in previous lessons. In addition, we'll create a drop cap and we'll make use of the layout checker in PagePlus.

Selecting a Template

1. As in our previous lessons that used a template, select Template in the StartUp Assistant window.

2. In the Open Template dialog, scroll to the Newsletters & Magazines category.

3. In the Template box, select `news2.ppt`, which is the multi-page newsletter template we'll work with. See Figure 15.1.

Importing Text

1. To change headlines and subheads, just highlight the text you want to change and type in the change. Resize the text to fit the space, if necessary. See Figure 15.2.

FIGURE 15.1 The `news2.ppt` newsletter template

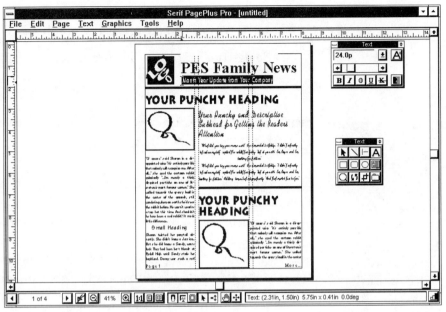

FIGURE 15.2 Highlighted text in subhead

2. To add text from an outside word processor, put the cursor where you want the text inserted, pull down the File menu, and click Import Text.

3. When you're asked if you want to Replace, Append, or Cancel, click on Replace.

4. Your text will automatically flow onto the template. If it's too long for the page, you'll be asked if you want it to automatically flow onto subsequent pages. Click Yes.

Importing Graphics

1. To change the graphics that are already in place on the template, click on the graphic you want to replace, pull down the File menu, and click on Import Picture.

2. When the Picture Assistant window pops up, select the source from which you'll import the graphic.

3. Select the graphic from the dialog and place it with the OLE tool.

➡ **PagePlus TIP**

Make sure you're not zoomed in or in 100% view mode, or you won't see any of the pasteboard. If none of the pasteboard is visible, click on the magnifying glass button with the minus sign (at the bottom of the PagePlus window). This will lower the view from 100% to 75% to 50% and so on.

Creating a Drop Cap

Effects such as drop caps can add a touch of class to your layout. PagePlus lets you create drop caps and add a border or color to them as well. But for now, we'll just add a simple drop cap.

As with almost anything you do on the computer, there are several ways to add a drop cap in PagePlus. The simplest is to work on the pasteboard. (The pasteboard is the area surrounding the page.)

1. Move your cursor over to the pasteboard area, and with the Text tool selected from the tool box, type the letter you want for a drop cap.

2. Select the letter and enlarge it to whatever point size you want the drop cap to be. Here we've chosen 40.1 points. See Figure 15.3.

FIGURE 15.3

Choosing a size for a drop cap

3. Select the Pointer tool, and you'll see eight little black boxes (handles) surrounding the letter. See Figure 15.4.

4. To get a better handle on the letter, click on the middle handle on the right and drag it in toward the letter. Let go of the mouse button. See Figure 15.5.

5. Pull down the Tools menu and click on Wrap Settings.

6. When the Wrap Settings window pops up, click on Wrap Outside. See Figure 15.6.

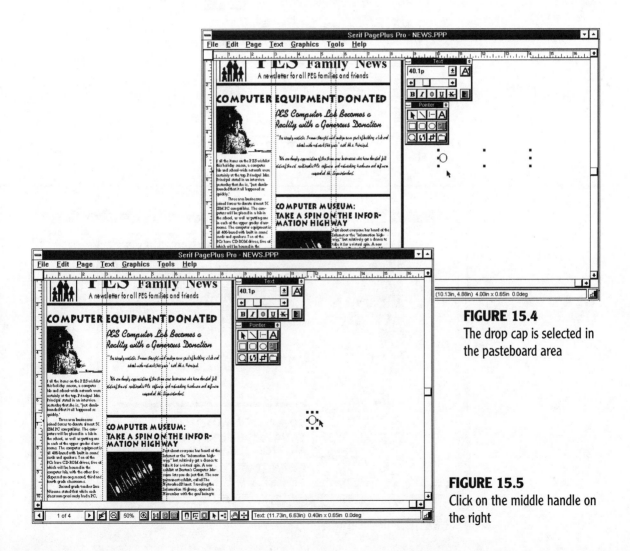

FIGURE 15.4
The drop cap is selected in the pasteboard area

FIGURE 15.5
Click on the middle handle on the right

→ **PagePlus TIP**
To get the text to wrap around the letter, click on the wrap line around the letter (the handles) and pull it out toward the text as much as you can.

7. Drag the letter over to the place in your text where you want the drop cap to be positioned. Let go of the mouse button when the top of the drop cap is aligned with the top of the other letters in the line. See Figure 15.7.

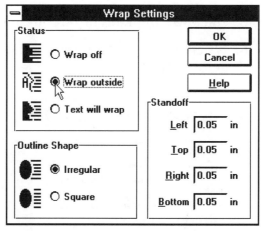

FIGURE 15.6 Choosing a wrap setting

FIGURE 15.7 Positioning a drop cap

Checking the Layout

1. When you're satisfied with your layout, it's time to let PagePlus check it for you. To do this, pull down the Tools menu and click on Layout Checker.

2. When the Layout Checker dialog pops up, type in the pages you want to check, or click All. See Figure 15.8.

3. Layout Checker will let you check for text alignment, blank pages, unused text, and more. You can tell Layout Checker to only check for specific things by clicking Options in the Layout Checker dialog. This will bring up the Layout Options dialog. (Note that we've checked everything here.) See Figure 15.9.

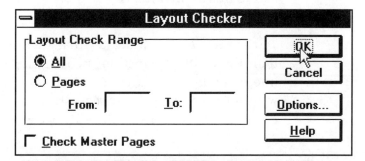

FIGURE 15.8
Selecting pages to check

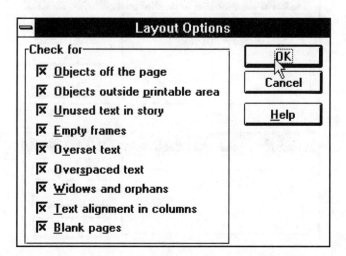

FIGURE 15.9
Choosing the Layout Checker options

4. Click on OK, and Layout Checker will check each page you asked it to.

When you use Layout Checker, it will more than likely find something wrong with your creation. Don't panic, and don't take it personally, either. Rely on your own design sense rather than assuming that Layout Checker is right and your design is wrong. Layout Checker is similar to a grammar and spelling checker, which are only as good at grammar and spelling as the person using it. The following are a few common problems that Layout Checker will find with your design. Also suggested are a few simple solutions to remedy these situations, if and when they need to be remedied.

- *Unused text in story.* This can be remedied by going to the text in the selected frame (Layout Checker automatically selects the frame where the problem occurs) and deleting or editing text to fit. Another remedy is to add more pages to fit the text. See Figure 15.10.

- *Text is overset.* This indicates that there is text that is wider than the width specified for it. This may occur if you have a line made up of a single word or you enlarge a text object without increasing its text width accordingly. Fix this by changing the specified text width. See Figure 15.11.

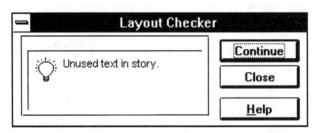

FIGURE 15.10
Layout Checker finds unused text

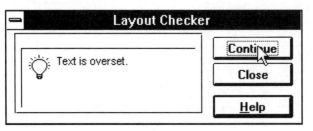

FIGURE 15.11
Layout Checker finds overset text

- *Overspaced text.* This is text with word spaces that are larger than the maximum word space value set. Correct this by hyphenating words to change the lengths of the lines. See Figure 15.12.

- *Text lines in consecutive columns don't line up.* This indicates that the lines of text in adjacent column frames do not line up. The remedy for this is simply to add to the text or edit it to make it fit. In many cases, columns that end in different places are exactly what you want in your design, so you don't need to fix a thing. See Figure 15.13.

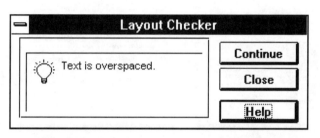

FIGURE 15.12
Layout Checker finds overspaced text

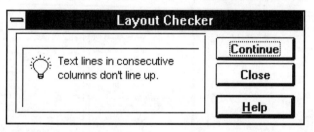

FIGURE 15.13
Layout Checker finds misaligned columns

Outputting the Newsletter

Like any desktop publishing project, newsletters can be printed on your desktop printer, in black and white or in color if you have a color printer. If you want to go one step up from a complete do-it-yourselfer, take your newsletter to a professional printer or service bureau. But before taking the job out of house, print a dummy copy. You can choose to suppress the pictures; placeholders will show

PES Family News
A newsletter for all PES families and friends

COMPUTER EQUIPMENT DONATED

PES Computer Lab Becomes a Reality with a Generous Donation

"I'm simply tickled. I can accept all we've received of building a lab and lab-wide network this year" said Mrs. Principal.

"We can't really appreciate it. I feel we can accomplish a real thing all kinds of spectacular PCs software and networking, hardware and software supplied Mr. Superintendent.

Of all the items on the PES wishlist this holiday season, a computer lab and school-wide network were certainly at the top. Principal Mrs. Principal stated in an interview yesterday that she is, "just dumbfounded that it all happened so quickly."

Three area businesses joined forces to donate almost 50 IBM PC compatibles. The computer will be placed in a lab in the school, as well as putting one in each of the upper grade classrooms. The computer equipment is all 486-based with built in sound cards and speakers. Ten of the PCs have CD-ROM drives, five of which will be housed in the computer lab, with the other five dispersed among second, third and fourth grade classrooms.

Second grade teacher Ima Wizann stated that while each classroom previously had a PC

COMPUTER MUSEUM: TAKE A SPIN ON THE INFORMATION HIGHWAY

Just about everyone has heard of the Internet or the "information highway," but relatively got a chance to take it for a virtual spin. A new exhibit at Barton's Computer Museum lets you do just that. The new permanent exhibit, called The Networked Planet Traveling the Information Highway, opened in November with the goal being to

Page 1   More...

STUDENTS LINE UP FOR FUN
Computer Lab Draws a Crowd

Of all the items on the PES wishlist this holiday season, a computer lab and school-wide network were certainly at the top. Principal Mrs. Principal stated in an interview yesterday that she is, "just dumbfounded that it all happened so quickly."

Three area businesses joined forces to donate almost 50 IBM PC compatibles. The computer will be placed in a lab in the school, as well as putting one in each of the upper grade classrooms. The computer equipment is all 486-based with built in sound

cards and speakers. Ten of the PCs have CD-ROM drives, five of which will be housed in the computer lab, with the other five dispersed among second, third and fourth grade classrooms.

Second grade teacher Ima Wizann stated that while each classroom previously had a PC, none of them had PCs with enough memory to run the latest software. "So many new software titles are available these days, and with our old equipment, we couldn't run them. Many of the kids had better equipment at home and thought of the school equipment as being from the dinosaur age."

Fourth grade student Joe Technical added that, "Finally we've got some real iron in here. I've taken apart our old system so

FIELD TRIP OF THE MONTH

Computer Museum Visitors Take a Spin on the Information

Just about everyone has heard of the Internet or the "information highway," but relatively got a chance to take it for a virtual spin. A new exhibit at Barton's Computer Museum lets you do

just that. The new permanent exhibit, called The Networked Planet Traveling the Information Highway, opened in November with the goal being to "make the invisible visible," according to David Gruchler, Director of Exhibits

By becoming a network user, visitors to the exhibit learn first-hand the role of global networking. A fun game that familiar can play together on the network is to play fund manager on the world trading market. With $1 million in the hands of

Page 2   More...

TEACHER SPOT

"Of course," said Sharon in a disappointed voice "It's entirely possible that nobody will recognize me. After all..." she eyed the cartoon rabbit quizzically "...I'm merely a thinly disguised pastiche on one of literature's most famous women." She walked towards the grassy knoll in the center of the grounds, still wondering where on earth she'd seen the rabbit before. He wasn't wearing a top hat

"What did you say your name was?" she demanded irritably. "I didn't actually introduce myself," replied the fox Jessica." Adding somewhat enigmatically "And that makes two so far.'

New Faces

Sharon twisted her ponytail absently. She didn't know a Jessica. But she did know a Sandy, worse luck. They had been best friends at Rydell High until Sandy stole her boyfriend. Danny was such a rat She sighed in remembrance. It was a world away from the mysterious garden and the cartoon rabbit. (How did she get here? Last thing she remembered she'd been in a Chrysler, as big as a whale, heading down the Atlanta highway, looking for a love getaway.) She was puzzled by the rabbit's reply. "I've

ANNUAL DUCK RACE

Get Your Duckies Lined Up!

"Of course," said Sharon in a disappointed voice "It's entirely possible that nobody will recognize me. After all..." she eyed the cartoon rabbit quizzically "...I'm merely a thinly disguised pastiche on one of literature's most famous women." She walked towards the grassy knoll in the center of the grounds, still wondering where on earth she'd seen the rabbit before. He wasn't wearing a top hat this time Shouldn't he have been a real live rabbit? It made little difference...

that nobody will recognize me. After all..." she eyed the cartoon rabbit quizzically "...I'm merely a thinly disguised pastiche on one of literature's most famous women." She walked toward the grassy knoll in the center of the grounds, still wondering where on earth she'd seen the rabbit before. He

Sharon twisted her ponytail absently. She didn't know a Sandy worse luck. They had been best friends at Rydell High until Sandy stole her boyfriend. Danny was such a rat! She sighed in remembrance. It was a world away from this mysterious garden and the cartoon rabbit. (How did she get

Page 3   More...

Quips...

"Of course" said Sharon in a disappointed voice "It's entirely possible that nobody will recognize me. After all..." she eyed the cartoon rabbit quizzically "...I'm merely a thinly disguised pastiche on one of literature's most famous women." She walked towards the grassy knoll in the center of the grounds, still wondering where on earth she'd seen the rabbit before. He wasn't wearing a top hat this time. And shouldn't he have been a real live rabbit? It made little difference to the puzzle.

and more quips

"What did you say your name was?" she demanded irritably. "I didn't actually introduce myself," replied the rabbit tearfully "but or you ask; I'm Roger, and I'm looking for Jessica." Adding somewhat enigmatically "And that makes two so far."

Sharon twisted her ponytail absently. She didn't know a Jessica. But she did know a Sandy, worse luck. They had been best friends at Rydell High until Sandy stole her boyfriend. Danny was such a rat! She sighed in remembrance. It was a world away from the mysterious garden and the rabbit. (How did she get here? Last thing she remembered she'd been in a Chrysler heading down the Atlanta highway, looking for a low

BUS DUTY UPDATE

"Of course" said Sharon in a disappointed voice "It's entirely possible that nobody will recognize me. After all..." she eyed the cartoon rabbit quizzically "...I'm merely a thinly disguised pastiche on one of the grounds, still wandering where on earth she'd seen the rabbit before He wasn't wearing a top hat this time. And shouldn't he have been a real live rabbit? It made little difference to the puzzle.

Driver of the Month

"What did you say your name was?" she demanded irritably. "I didn't actually introduce myself," replied the rabbit tearfully "but as you ask; I'm Roger, and I'm looking for Jessica." Adding somewhat enigmatically "And that makes two so far.'

Sharon twisted her ponytail absently. She didn't know a Jessica. But she did know a Sandy, worse luck. They had been best friends at Rydell High until Sandy stole her boyfriend. Danny was such a rat! Shouldn't he have been a real live rabbit from the mysterious garden and the rabbit. (How did she get here? Last thing she remembered she'd been in a Chrysler heading down the Atlanta highway, looking for a low

PES FAMILY NEWS
PHONE 1-800-999-9999
FAX 1-800-999-9999

Printed by Grove Press with design by
Hilltop Design
Edited by I.M. Bright
Written by Gotta Babble

Page 4   More...

FIGURE 15.14 The finished newsletter

where the graphics should be positioned. You can also print thumb-nails of the newsletter. Thumbnails can contain as many as eight pages of your newsletter on each sheet. This gives you a convenient way to check your layout on paper.

If you're having your newsletter printed on anything but a standard size paper, include crop marks to show the printer the size you want your publication trimmed to.

Stepping Out

In the process of mastering the basics of desktop publishing, you've probably run up against some pretty fancy publishing and design terms that mean next to nothing to you. Many of these terms are explained here. The details of color printing are discussed, along with a discussion of how to prepare camera-ready copy, how to use photographs, clip art, and other images, and how to use the Serif add-ons to PagePlus. Like Part I, Part III is intended to be used long after you've mastered the basics of PagePlus or any other program. These final two chapters provide you with the knowledge you need to begin to delve into the intricacies of desktop publishing and to achieve the kind of results that, until now, you have only dreamed of achieving.

Advanced Stuff

Color

Most desktop publishing programs make it simple enough to add color, and if you have your own color printer, you don't need to think too much about it. But once you step over the threshold of your own office and send your work out to a commercial printer or service bureau, you'll be confronted with lingo that may be unfamiliar to you. You don't need to become an expert on color printing, but knowing what the different types of colors are and how they are printed will help you communicate better with your printer—and better communication will result in a better end product.

First of all, if you've worked with color at all on your computer, you've probably noticed that what you see on-screen is *not* what you get on paper. One difference is that screen colors are generated from red, green, and blue (commonly referred to as RGB color). Printed colors are made up of cyan, magenta, yellow, and black (called CMYK color). RGB colors are bright; CMYK colors are often deeper and darker. The way the colors are produced differs as well. Colors on your computer screen are produced by different wavelengths of light, while printed colors are made from combinations of actual color pigments.

Process Color

Process color is composed of cyan, magenta, yellow, and black, combined in different percentages to form just about every color imaginable. In the abbreviation CMYK, C is for cyan, M is for magenta, Y is for yellow, and K is for black. (K is used for black instead of B because

B might be interpreted as blue.) Each color is applied as a percentage, with 10 percent increments being standard. To change a color, for example, you might keep adding yellow in 10 percent increments until you achieve the desired color.

Process colors vary from source to source, so if you're generating process color for a publication, it should all be done on the same system in order to get a consistent output. This means that you should not only have an entire job printed at the same place, but should also check the color carefully when you get a proof. Sometimes two colors from the same system may not match perfectly.

To create or match process colors, get a book that shows the various screen combinations. Most books show screens in increments of 10 percent, though it is possible to apply screens in 5 percent or even 1 percent increments.

You'll hear the term "register" used in reference to four-color printing. This applies to the alignment of the four color screens. If the colors are not correctly aligned, you'll get a blurry image. You've probably seen this effect in mass-produced department store fliers. There's no reason for the register to be off—someone should check the print quality of the final output.

To help avoid register problems, you can allow some amount of "trap," or overlap of colors. If you don't allow enough trap, you'll get a thin white line at one side of the graphic or the other, where the colors don't meet.

Another problem that can occur in printing process colors is the creation of "moire" patterns. This happens when overlapping screens form a pattern. You can help eliminate moire patterns by removing as much black as possible from your desktop publishing creations. You may also want to try rotating the screens to see if that gets rid of the pattern.

> **➡ PagePlus TIP**
>
> In PagePlus, you can set the trap value in the Color Separation dialog. From the Print dialog, click on Color, then in the Color Separation dialog, click on Settings.

Spot Color

Spot color is not made up of CMYK, but is instead just a single color. It is often used for projects that require just one color. For example, if you designed a business card with a logo in one color, you could ask the printer to use spot color. Spot color can also be used in addition to process color, thus adding a fifth color. Spot color is simpler and easier for commercial printers to work with than process color. The printer makes a negative for each color used; if the colors don't touch each other, the printer doesn't have to separate them. If the colors do touch or overlap, separation is necessary.

When sending a job with spot color to a printer, it's a good idea to print a sample on your printer, even if your printer is only black and white. This way you can supply the printer with the file and also with a sample showing where the color should be applied.

Pantone colors are common spot colors. PagePlus and other desktop publishing programs give you access to Pantone colors.

Pantone Colors

If you want to be sure of what you're going to get in print, you can choose a standard Pantone color from a book. While the color may not look perfect on-screen, the printed color will match what you've chosen.

Pantone colors are premixed using a specific formula. The colors are catalogued in Pantone Matching Books, which you can flip through to find your color of choice. You then enter its corresponding Pantone Matching System (PMS) number into your computer.

Printing

The easiest and perhaps cheapest way of "printing in color" is to print black ink on colored paper. A step up from that is to print on a desktop color ink-jet or laser printer. Your next option—the one that will give you the most professional results—is to go to your handy neighborhood commercial printer.

Printing in Color

When it's time to print your creation, you can print it to a file and ask your desktop publishing program to color-separate it for you.

This will give you four files, one for each color. For the best results, take these files to a service bureau where they can be output as film. Then take the film to a commercial printer for printing. You can, of course, print your creation on your own desktop color printer, but this will most likely give you a print quality of 300 DPI, or at best 600 DPI. A service bureau can give you 1200 DPI, 2400 DPI, or higher, on film or on paper.

If your desktop publishing creation consists of a lot of type that will be printed in a single color, along with a few full-color graphics, you'll probably want to send just the graphics to a service bureau for film output. You can have your commercial printer "strip" this film into your publication.

When you decide to take your work to a commercial printer, camera-ready art is what you need, no matter which route you take to produce it or what format is sent to the printer (plain paper, floppy disks, or mechanicals). You have two options for producing camera-ready art. One is to output your creation on your own desktop printer (at the highest resolution possible). The second option is to send the file (or files) to a service bureau and have them output to paper. You then take the paper copy to your commercial printer for shooting and film output.

For your work to be truly camera ready, it must adhere to these basic principles:

- All type and art is in place.

- All elements are as they should appear in the final document, with no special instructions for text or graphics.

- The desired page size is the same as what is being shot.

Mechanical Paste-Up

In the days prior to electronic publishing, type and graphics were output separately and manually pasted down onto boards. The result of this process is called a mechanical. Some printers will print from a file on a floppy disk, but many still prefer to be handed a camera-ready mechanical. If handing the printer a floppy disk won't do, you can still go the mechanical route with your desktop-printed output. Simply paste down the output (printed on a laser printer at the highest resolution possible) onto a mechanical board. Pasting your output to a board will keep it from being bent or torn, and adding a sheet of tracing paper over it will keep it from being smudged with fingerprints. You can buy boards with light blue rules that are specially designed for use as mechanicals. Light blue doesn't reproduce when shot by a camera; you can use these lines to help you line up the copy.

If you do go the mechanical route, you can (and should) do a few things to get the best reproduction possible. First, use a very white paper. If printing from a laser printer, use special laser printer paper. If you're going to produce a lot of mechanicals, you might want to invest in a wax machine for attaching the paper to the board. If you're not going into mechanical production full-time, you can just use rubber cement. A spray adhesive is available as well, but because it is toxic, we are not recommending that you use it.

Be sure to include these things on each mechanical:

- crop marks

- page numbers

- placement for spot colors

- information about the addition of graphics that are not included on the mechanical

You can include this information right on the tracing paper overlay. If you do have graphics that the printer will strip in, indicate where they go with boxes on the mechanical. Write FPO ("for position only") in the boxes. Let the printer know if you want a border around a graphic, even if you've included it on your desktop-printed output. The printer can use a line marking a border for positioning and can then mask it out.

Find out what other information the printer needs for your particular job. Communicating as much information as possible beforehand will ensure the best output.

Offset Printing

Anything you print is printed in at least one "color," even if it's black. Two-color printing refers to the use of two inks, rather than two colors (inks can be mixed to create colors). And, naturally, four-color printing refers to using four inks. Most commercial printers use offset lithography. The way this works is, you bring your camera-ready art to the printer, and he or she takes a photo of it. That image is then transferred onto a plate, which is put on a press. The plate is inked, and it transfers the image to a rubber mat called a blanket. The blanket then transfers, or offsets, the image onto the paper.

To get more than one color, the printer has to run the paper through the press more than one time in order to apply additional colors of ink. It's always a good idea to give your printer enough time to run the print job, *and* to give yourself enough time to check for any errors. And the printer will need additional time to correct any errors that you might find. Errors can include images that are out of register, moire patterns, trapping problems, and more.

Camera-ready art given to a printer should include clear instructions on the following:

- where to add color

- where to trim or fold

- what paper to use

- ink colors

- number of copies needed

- any other special instructions

Be specific about how many printed copies you need. Printers often have a policy that allows them to print slightly more or less than what is on the print order (because it is difficult to exactly gauge the speed of an offset press, and it is expensive to restart a press once it has stopped). Make sure you know exactly what you need and communicate it to the printer.

Finally, before your job is printed, ask to see a blueline proof. This is a sample print made from the negative they'll use to create the printing plates for your job. Check the blueline for the following:

- The artwork is in place.

- The publication is trimmed and folded correctly.

- All type and graphics are in the correct position.

- The pages are in the right order.

- There are no smudges or dust marks that may show up in the final output.

- There is no broken type.

You can't check color on a blueline, so if color is critical to your piece or if you've asked for complex color work, pay a little extra to get a color proof.

Adobe OPI Specs

Many desktop publishing programs let you include comments about PostScript files. These comments refer to a set of specifications set by Adobe Corporation, called the Open Prepress Interface (OPI). The OPI lets you send information about imported bitmap images to OPI-compatible systems. OPI specs control the placement, size, rotation, and cropping of imported bitmap pictures. Be sure to find out if your service bureau needs OPI comments included with the files you send for production. To include them, your dtp software lets you specify OPI comments when you print a document (whether you print to paper or to a file). In PagePlus you click Option on the Print dialog, and check the Include OPI Comments box.

Working with a Service Bureau

Service bureaus are in the business of taking your files and turning them into 35-millimeter slides, overhead transparencies, or paper or film for reproduction by a professional printer. You can print your own work, but the resolution will be limited to whatever your desktop printer can produce. Most often this is only 300 DPI, which is good enough for some desktop publishing work, but not for artwork or text that needs a professional look. Service bureaus print pages at resolutions of 1200 DPI and higher. The output is on glossy photographic paper or on film, depending on how you'll be reproducing it.

To find a good service bureau, ask around. One of the best ways of finding a good service bureau is through word of mouth. Look for a service bureau that will cater to your needs and adhere to your specifications.

In the past, most desktop publishing was done on the Macintosh. Service bureaus got used to working with Mac files only, and some have not updated their equipment to handle files from IBM PCs and compatible systems. In addition, some service bureaus aren't used to working with Windows-based files. Find a service bureau with a reputation for having state-of-the-art equipment and experience with PC files. Chances are, the service bureau will work with your file on a Mac if they can open it on one. For example, if you save your PagePlus creation in a standard file format such as TIFF (Tagged-Image File Format) or EPS, the service bureau should be able to open it either on a Mac or a PC.

The problem with a service bureau's using, for example, PageMaker and Illustrator on a PC is that, while these programs run on both PCs and Macs, Windows handles type fonts differently than a Mac. In many cases a particular Windows font does not match the Mac font of the same name. Don't expect a service bureau to have PagePlus; however, you should expect them to alert you if their fonts don't match yours. Some service bureaus will let you choose a font they do have, to use as a substitute for yours (for a fee, of course).

The location of a service bureau isn't of great importance to everyone. It is important, however, if you want to go there to check the output or if you want to pick up and deliver materials. On the other hand, if you're sending files and have a modem, you can transmit your files electronically to most service bureaus. They can send you your output via a messenger service for next day delivery. Look in the Yellow Pages under typesetting or desktop publishing to find service bureaus in your area.

Before you send a large or important job to a service bureau, run a test. Send them a file from your PC and see what they can do with it. If you can print it, they should be able to. Run a test for yourself first, just to make sure that your creation is indeed printable.

When you work with a service bureau, you'll need to communicate the following information to them:

- what computer and program you used to create your files (for example, an IBM PC running PagePlus 3.0)

- what you want the service bureau to output (that is, the name of the document, number of pages, and so on)

- what typefaces you used in the files you want the service bureau to produce

- what type of output you want (film or paper)

- what size output you want (should it be enlarged or reduced?)

- what DPI you want the job output at (i.e., 1200 or 2400 DPI).

Photography, Clip Art, and Other Images

PagePlus comes with clip art arranged by subject matter. We have used some of this clip art in the hands-on lessons in this book to illustrate our desktop publishing creations. There are many vendors that sell additional clip art on disk or CD. These are just a few of the many ways you can include photographs and other graphics in your creations. Other methods include scanning images, using digital photography, and using screen-capture programs. You can decide what's best for you based on what hardware you already have, what type of clip art or graphics you need or have, and what your skills are at this point. Using methods such as digital photography and photograph scanning involves investing in a new piece of hardware. As with any new hardware, this will require an additional investment on your part in learning to use the equipment and having it perform the way you want it to. Other options, such as clip art, Photo CDs, and screen-captures, make use of equipment that you probably already have (assuming that you have a CD-ROM drive). Let's examine each of these methods of image input now.

Clip Art

Clip art is one of the lowest-cost ways of adding graphics to your desktop publishing creations. PagePlus comes with a lot of useful clip art, but if you're planning to use it extensively you may want to look into other sources, because you'll soon exhaust the PagePlus library. See the resources in Appendix C for clip art vendors.

 HINT

One caution—when ordering clip art, if you buy PostScript images, make sure you'll be outputting them on a PostScript device.

There are two types of clip art: bitmapped and object-oriented. Bitmapped images are made up of dots. They cost less, but they cannot be enlarged very well without showing jagged edges. You can, however, edit bitmapped images using an image- or photo-editing program. Object-oriented clip art lets you alter the size without distorting the image. The image is stored as a whole, rather than as dots.

Photo CDs

A Photo CD is a compact disc that contains scanned photographs that can be viewed on your computer. Kodak's Photo CD is the standard that most CD manufacturers follow today. This standard has been so widely accepted by manufacturers that most new CD-ROM drives can read images from Photo CD discs and most graphics and desktop publishing applications can open them, including PagePlus.

Using commercial Photo CDs is one way to go. (See the resource guide in Appendix C for specific vendors.) Another way is to have your own photos put on Photo CDs. One big drawback to this, however, is the cost. For example, you can get 24-exposure color or black-and-white print film processed in Photo CD format for just under $30, which is more than three times what it costs to get regular prints. You can also take negatives or slides to your local camera store, and for less than $2 per image get them scanned onto a Photo CD. According to Kodak, there are currently over thirty thousand photo finishers and service bureaus, including major department store chains, equipped to convert film, negatives, or slides to Photo CD format. For the Photo CD transfer service nearest you, call 800-235-6325.

Besides the fact that putting your photos on a CD puts them at your fingertips for all kinds of desktop publishing and other computer applications, one big advantage is that, assuming you have a CD-ROM drive, you don't need to purchase another hardware device (such as a scanner or a digital camera) to pull photos onto your desktop. Another advantage is that you can keep the images stored on the CD rather than putting them on your hard drive. Photographs and other high-resolution images can take up tens or hundreds of megabytes of space on your hard drive. Storing those monstrous files on CD makes sense!

Like CDs full of clip art images, the market is now flooded with Photo CDs with photographic images, such as Corel's Professional Photos and PhotoDisc's PhotoDisc Library. To use a Photo CD, all you need is a CD-ROM drive and the Photo CD.

Scanners

You can also add pizzazz to your desktop publishing creations by scanning in art or photographs. But before you think of adding a scanner to your desktop publishing studio, you should know what the two basic types of scanners are and how you can choose what's best for you.

Scanners work very much like copy machines. They both capture an image, but scanners go a step further and convert the image to digital form. The digital image is stored on your computer and is displayed as dots and lines on-screen. The sharpness of the image scanned is measured in dots per inch (DPI) and lines per inch (LPI). While it might seem that the higher the DPI and LPI the better the image, this is not necessarily true. What higher resolutions do produce, however, is a much larger file size. An image, for example, that is scanned at 300 DPI may take as much as 5 MB on your hard drive. Scan the same image at 600 DPI, and it'll occupy a whopping 20 MB! To store a few images of that size, you'd need an extra hard drive just for your graphics, which is the way many professional graphics studios work.

The two most common types of scanners are the flatbed scanner and the hand-held scanner. The flatbed works the most like the old copy machine. You lift the hood, place the photograph or document face down on the scanner, and the scanner reflects light off the document to record what is on the page. The hand-held scanner looks like a mini vacuum cleaner. You hold the scanner in your hand and take swipes across the page, and the scanner reads the part of the document you covered. You have to hold your hand steady, though, because you want those swipes to be consistent.

When choosing between a flatbed and a hand-held scanner, consider what kinds of images or documents you'll be scanning, what kinds of results you want, how often you'll use it, and how much space you have in your work area. If you'll be scanning images that are more than 4½ inches wide, and if the quality of the output is critical, opt for a flatbed. If, on the other hand, you'll rarely use a scanner, the output isn't critical, and you don't have much room left on your desk, you may want to go with a hand-held.

Hand-held scanners can be difficult to manipulate unless you have the most steady of hands. To successfully scan an 8½- by 11-inch document, you'd have to take two swipes down the page and then "stitch" the two scanned pieces together using software. Logitech's ScanMan is an example of a hand-held scanner with a built-in "auto-stitch" capability.

While gray-scale scanners (those that scan in shades of black and white only) are less expensive than color scanners, prices of color scanners have come down low enough to make the additional investment worth every penny for the improved quality you get. Note that owning a color scanner doesn't imply that you must output your scanned images in color or that you can scan only color images. A 24-bit color scanner actually gives you better results on black and white images as well.

As far as price goes, you can purchase a gray-scale flatbed for less than $500, while you can purchase a gray-scale hand-held for around $200. If you want color, add about $100 to the cost of the flatbed scanner and add about $200 to the cost of the hand-held.

Finally, there are two more items to consider. One is TWAIN compliance; the other is the software you need to run the scanner. TWAIN is simply an application-interface standard agreed to by the major manufacturers of software and input devices. Before TWAIN, each scanner manufacturer had to include its own software and drivers to run the scanner. You simply had to hope they were compatible with the other applications that you ran, such as Adobe PageMaker or QuarkXpress. With TWAIN, it's a one-step process. As long as the scanner is TWAIN-compliant, you should be able to run your scanner from within your application. This greatly simplifies the process of getting the image into your computer.

Most scanners come with OCR (optical character recognition) software, which interprets the text on a page and stores the information on your hard drive. Good-quality OCR software is capable of recognizing just about any text, regardless of typeface. Many scanners also come with photo-manipulation software, such as Adobe Photoshop, Adobe PhotoStyler, and Micrografx Picture Publisher or PhotoMagic for Windows, which let you edit the image once it's been scanned.

Digital Cameras

Like the Photo CD, the digital camera is suited to someone who wants to have full control over the creation of images, as well as instant results. And like today's color desktop scanners, digital cameras can produce 24-bit color images. Many of the cameras on the market today are small and lightweight (many weigh not much more than one pound).

Digital cameras such as Apple's QuickTake 100, Logitech's Fotoman Plus, and Dycam's Model 4 are fully automatic, point-and-shoot cameras. They are used in a manner similar to that of regular automatic cameras. Most come equipped with a standard 50-millimeter lens. What is different is the way the photos are stored.

Instead of loading film into the camera, you just point and shoot, and the image is stored in the camera's memory. The only thing you need to load are the batteries.

Naturally the camera's memory is limited, so you can take a maximum of thirty-two 8-bit pictures at a resolution of 320 by 240, or twenty-four 8-bit pictures at a resolution of 640 by 480. You can also mix up the resolutions and take some combination of each. To get the pictures out of the camera, first you save the images in one of many graphics-standard formats, such as BMP, PCX, or TIFF. Then you connect a serial cable between the camera and your computer, plugging one end into the camera and the other end into your printer or modem port. Using the software that comes with the camera, you download the images to your computer. Many of today's cameras, including the Apple QuickTake and the Logitech FotoMan Plus, include image-editing software that lets you view, crop, rotate, resize, and switch the color depth of the images. From there, as with other graphics images stored on your hard drive, you can use a photo-manipulation application for retouching and other effects.

Digital cameras offer you control over the images you capture. The outcome can be of as high a quality as you'll get from scanning or from importing a photo from a Photo CD, but you will be in full control—you take the image in the first place, and then you can manipulate it to your heart's content. Digital cameras range widely in price; you can find high-quality models, both color and black-and-white, for $700 and up.

Screen-Capture Programs

When you need to take a snapshot of what is on your computer screen, you need a screen-capture program. Many of the screen-capture programs on the market do a lot more than just take pictures of what is on your screen. In fact, screen-capture programs have become such handy utilities that no desktop publishing studio should be without one. Some let you change a graphics file from one format to another, some let you add boarders to graphics files, and others let you capture images not just on your PC screen but from scanners and Photo CDs as well.

One drawback to many screen-capture programs is that only capture Windows screens and not DOS screens, so you have to be running a Windows application in order to capture a screen. Inset Systems' HiJaak Pro is one, however, that is capable of capturing in DOS.

When you choose a screen-capture program, make sure that it captures the file formats you're most likely to need. In addition, remember that file formats are updated from time to time, and an earlier format may not be what you need. For example, TIFF is now in its sixth revision in eight years. The first version supported black and white only. Version 6.0 supports black and white, gray-scales, various color depths, and more. Most screen-capture utilities on the market today capture the latest and the greatest of the file formats, but just make sure the one you buy captures those you need most. If your screen-capture program is old, you may find yourself trying to open a file that's in a new format that is not supported by your utility. Not all of them, for instance, capture Photo CD–format files.

Prices of screen-capture software range from nearly free (for shareware) up to $200 or more. Some of the lower priced products, such as Clip 'n Save from Dynalink Technologies, simply capture screens in a variety of formats, while the higher-end utilities, such as Inner Media's Collage PM, support a wide range of file formats and offer image-processing capabilities, image-management functions, and special printing functions.

Photo Editing

Once you've captured the image you want to use, you may want to change its color or size, or you may want to crop it or rotate it. You can do all this and more with photo-manipulation software such as Adobe Photoshop, Adobe PhotoStyler, Corel PhotoPaint, and Micrografx Picture Publisher or PhotoMagic for Windows. While the

high-end packages are popular, if you simply want to add some finishing touches to an image, spending $400 may be out of the ques-
tion. PhotoPaint and PhotoMagic are lower-cost programs that sell
for about a quarter of the price, but let you do just about everything
their high-end brothers can do.

Chapter 17

PagePlus Add-Ons

Serif PagePlus is a stand-alone desktop publishing program that comes with clip art, fonts, and the capability to produce a number of special effects. But there are some things you may want to do that you can't do with PagePlus alone. For example, you may want to edit a photo or add a drawing or a table. To accomplish these tasks you need an add-on package. Serif offers seven add-ons to help you get your work done without leaving the familiar PagePlus interface. All the add-ons work with PagePlus, as well as with other Windows applications. So before turning to a product by another vendor, you may want to try out one of Serif's low-cost add-ons. We'll cover the fundamentals of each add-on here to give you an idea of what its capabilities are.

ArtPacks

With PagePlus you can import pictures of just about any type from just about any source. PagePlus comes with a small selection of clip art to get you started. Serif's add-on ArtPacks come with over 500 pictures in a wide range of categories. You won't see the same art elsewhere, because the art in Serif's ArtPacks is created by professional artists at Serif.

Many of the images in the ArtPacks are in color. The images are fully scalable vector graphics stored as Windows metafiles (WMFs). In addition to graphic images and cartoons, you'll find useful page elements such as arrows, borders, and graduated backgrounds. There are also many business-type symbols, such as maps and diagrams for reports and presentations.

Installing ArtPacks

Each ArtPack takes about 8 MB of space on your hard drive. To install an ArtPack, you need to be running PagePlus or another Windows desktop publishing program, word processor, or spreadsheet.

The following are the different ArtPacks:

Entertainment	Toolkits 1 & 2
Food	Transport
Holidays	Travel
Home	Background Borders
Natural World	Decorative Borders
Office and Technology	Themed Borders
People	Miscellaneous
Sports	

The next time you import a picture, you'll see that the art has been installed in the Arts & Borders subdirectory. Scroll through the new graphics to see what they look like in the preview area of the dialog. This way you can see if you're importing a black-and-white or color image and if it's the image you want.

Using ArtPack Graphics

Since ArtPack images are Windows metafiles, you can use them with any Windows application that lets you import WMF files. Examples of applications that let you use ArtPacks include Lotus Ami Pro, Microsoft Publisher, Microsoft Word, and Adobe PageMaker.

You can modify ArtPack images in many ways. Almost any application will let you place the art anywhere you want it, and you can resize it as well. Most desktop publishing programs and some other applications will also let you crop an ArtPack image, so you use just the part you want from it. Still other applications, including PagePlus, will let you rotate an image and change its color. If you want to make more extensive changes to an image, import it to a Windows drawing program.

Designing with ArtPack Graphics

In Chapter 3 we covered many of the elements of good design, including the use of charts, clip art, and graphics. We also discussed the use of white space and keeping the design simple. This point cannot be emphasized enough. Desktop publishing makes it possible for anyone to become a designer and publisher, but some of the designs that get printed these days look as if the designer were sampling each and every font and graphic available. The following are a few key rules to keep in mind when designing with clip art and other images:

1. When you're placing a graphic on a page, make sure that it has a good reason for being there. Don't place a graphic on a page just to fill white space. In some instances the page would be better off with the white space left as it is.

2. Limit the number of typefaces or illustrations on a single page. Don't be tempted to show off all the art and fonts you have at your fingertips.

3. Use ornate borders only with plain or simple fonts. Likewise, surround fancy fonts with simple plain borders.

4. Keep your styles consistent. For example, don't combine a photographic image on a page with a cartoonish line drawing.

5. Ensure that your graphics will print well by making sure that you have the latest Windows driver installed for your printer and running a test.

DrawPlus

With PagePlus and other desktop publishing programs, there will be times when you want to do more to text or graphics than the application can handle. DrawPlus is an add-on vector drawing program that lets you create original artwork, recolor and customize Windows metafile images, and more.

Installing DrawPlus

DrawPlus requires at least a 286 system with 2 MB of RAM, and Windows 3.1 or higher running in standard or enhanced mode. Serif recommends that you have a 386SX or higher with at least 3 MB of RAM. DrawPlus uses about 1 MB of space on your hard drive.

To OLE or Not to OLE

DrawPlus can be used as an ordinary application or as an OLE applet. (An applet is a Windows application that you load with another Windows application.) As an ordinary application, you use it in the same way you would any other Windows program. For example, you follow these steps:

1. Start DrawPlus by clicking on its icon in the Program Manager window.

2. Create a drawing and save it as a DrawPlus file (use a **DPP** extension).

To edit the drawing at a later date, you have to start DrawPlus, reload the **DPP** file, edit it, and then save it again. If you want to use the drawing in a document, you have to copy it to the clipboard and then select Edit and Paste Special in the other application.

Using DrawPlus as an OLE applet has many advantages over using it as an ordinary Windows application. If you have a drawing that you will want to update regularly, OLE is the way to go. To use DrawPlus as an OLE applet, do this:

1. Start DrawPlus from its icon.

2. Create the drawing.

3. Click on the Update button, which puts a copy of the drawing in the Windows clipboard.

4. Switch back to your word processor or other program.

5. Select Edit and then Paste, which will paste in the drawing.

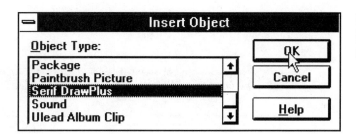

FIGURE 17.1

Importing an object
from DrawPlus

From within PagePlus, do this:

1. Pull down the Edit menu and click on Insert Object.

2. When the Insert Object dialog pops up, select the application from which you want to insert the object. Here we've selected Serif's DrawPlus. See Figure 17.1.

3. Create your drawing.

4. Exit DrawPlus and your drawing will be in position in your document. An alternative is to choose Update, which updates your publication but does not exit DrawPlus.

Using DrawPlus

When you click on the DrawPlus icon, you get the DrawPlus work screen, as shown in Figure 17.2.

The preview window shows you what your current drawing looks like. You create drawings in this window by selecting tools and clicking to use them in the window. When the cursor is over the window, it changes to show you which tool is selected.

The status bar shows you what is selected and how far you are zoomed in.

The front panel has most of the controls you need to create or alter your drawing. At the top are tools that let you create and manipulate objects. The second group down on the panel lets you change the attributes of any text object in your drawing. The third group lets you arrange objects, turn snapping on or off, flip objects, set the outline of an object, and set the document size. The last group lets you change the color of an object.

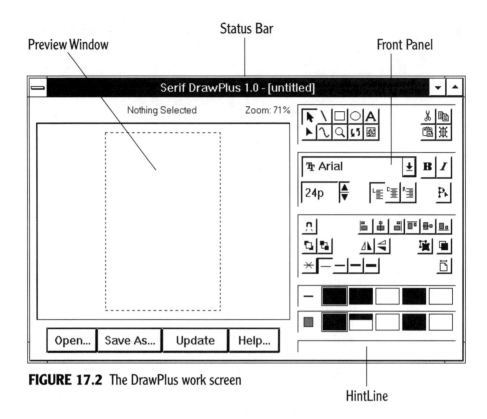

FIGURE 17.2 The DrawPlus work screen

The way you add text and create boxes, lines, ovals, and such is very similar to how these things are done in PagePlus. Even importing graphics and moving, sizing, and copying objects is done just as it is in PagePlus.

Two things you can do with DrawPlus that you can't do with PagePlus are change an object's outline and change its fill style. To change an object's outline:

1. Select an object using the Pointer tool.

2. Click on one of the Line Weight buttons.

3. Click on the Outline Color buttons. As you click on the buttons, the color of the object's outline changes.

HINT
Experiment with creating new colors and fills for your drawings.

To change an object's fill style:

1. Select an object using the Pointer tool.

2. Click on the Fill Style buttons. As you click on these buttons, the fill style of the object changes. Double-clicking on one of the buttons will bring up the Fill Style dialog, which will let you assign a new fill style to that button.

FontPacks

PagePlus comes with a selection of common typefaces for your use. These, however, are only a small sampling of the thousands of typefaces available. The typeface you choose for a desktop publishing creation will have a major impact on the overall look and feel of your publication. You can choose decorative typefaces for logos, invitations, posters, and so on or a simple sans serif font when you want your text to look straightforward. (Sans serif means that the letters do not have fancy little strokes at the ends.) There are typefaces that look computer-generated, and others that look like handwriting. Whatever mood you want to set, there's a typeface for that mood. If you don't find the typeface you want in PagePlus, you can add fonts from a Serif FontPack or use fonts from other vendors.

FontPacks are collections of 120 TrueType fonts that you can use with PagePlus and all of your other Windows 3.1 applications.

Installing FontPacks

Installing fonts for use in any Windows application is a simple process. To install new fonts, do the following:

1. Double-click on the Windows Control Panel icon.

2. Run Font Manager by double-clicking on the Fonts icon. See Figure 17.3.

3. Click on the Add button. Then select the drive that contains the FontPack disk.

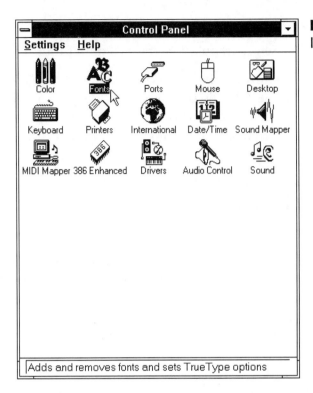

FIGURE 17.3
Installing fonts

 HINT
If you choose Select All and some of the fonts are already installed, you'll get a message telling you to uninstall the fonts before you can install new versions.

4. Select the fonts you want to add, or click on the Select All button.

5. Click the OK button.

PhotoPlus

PhotoPlus is a photo-editing program that works with PagePlus and other Windows applications. It lets you perform gamma correction; adjust color balance, brightness, and contrast; and rotate, flip, and crop. (Gamma refers to the changes in brightness of an image when you color correct it. Gamma is important depending on how you will output the image. For example, television monitors are normally brighter than computer monitors, and because Photo CD images are optimized for display on television monitors, you may need to gamma-correct the picture for display on your computer monitor). It also offers a range of special effects and patterns. You can emboss, poster-ize, and pixelize your pictures. You can solarize them and enhance their shadows and highlights. You can even make them look as if they were drawn by hand. There's also a set of digital processing filters for added effects.

PhotoPlus supports TWAIN scanners and the Kodak Photo CD format, so you can load and save pictures from just about every standard format there is and convert between them. Like DrawPlus, PhotoPlus can also work as an OLE applet.

Installing PhotoPlus

To run PhotoPlus, you need at least a 286 system with 2 MB of RAM running Windows in standard mode. Serif recommends that you have a 386SX or better with 3 MB of RAM and run Windows in enhanced mode. For optimal use, your PC should be configured with Windows to display at least 256 colors. PhotoPlus takes up about 1 MB of space on your hard drive.

Using PhotoPlus

As with DrawPlus, you can use PhotoPlus (Figure 17.4) as an ordinary application or as an OLE applet. See the preceding section on DrawPlus for a description of each.

PhotoPlus works with bitmapped graphics or photographs; this gives you a range of conversion and image-processing options, including the following:

- convert from one picture type to another (which you may want to do if your application doesn't support one type, such as JPEG)

- rotate or flip an image

- perform color correction, which can include adjusting the brightness, contrast, or color balance of a photograph

- crop parts of a picture

- add photo effects such as pixelized, poster-ized, and random-ized colors

Pixelizing refers to a process that makes a picture almost unrecognizable, as if you were looking at it through a frosted window. The process distorts the picture by replacing square groups of pixels with pixels of the average color of all the pixels in the original group. You can only pixelize 24-bit, true-color pictures, but PhotoPlus will convert a picture to true-color format if you try to use this method on a picture in another format.

Posterizing refers to making a photograph look as if it were painted on a poster, in a smaller number of colors rather than in full color. Posterizing often works better if you smooth the picture first.

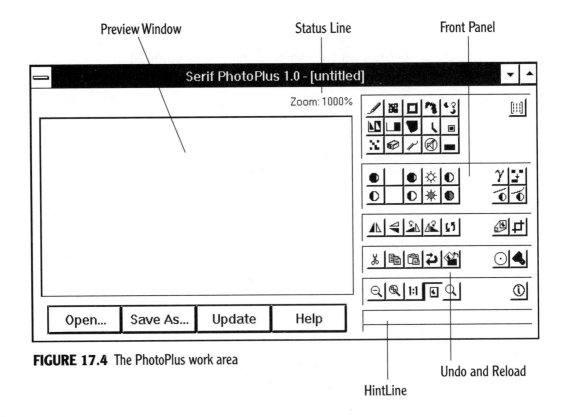

FIGURE 17.4 The PhotoPlus work area

Smoothing reduces the number of small, isolated, single-color areas. With PhotoPlus you can only posterize 8-bit, 256-color pictures (but you can also convert a picture to that format, if necessary).

Randomizing refers to creating a pop-art effect. Each color is changed to another color—randomly. This works best with a limited number of colors, so you might want to try posterizing the picture first.

Solarizing a photo refers to distorting the picture by inverting the brightest parts of the picture.

Like in DrawPlus, the preview window in PhotoPlus contains the picture you are working on. As you click buttons on the front panel, you will see the changes reflected in the picture. Don't forget about the Undo and Reload button. If you experiment too much and don't like the results, you can restore the original picture with a click of this button.

TablePlus

When you need to create tables quickly for inclusion in any Windows application, TablePlus can do the job. This table editor looks like a mini-spreadsheet and includes quick format and quick fill options. You can also rotate text in a cell or enter math calculations.

Installing TablePlus

To run TablePlus you need at least a 286 with 2 MB of RAM, running Windows in standard mode. Serif recommends that you have a 386SX or better system with at least 3 MB of RAM, running Windows in enhanced mode. TablePlus takes about 1 MB of space on your hard drive.

Using TablePlus

TablePlus works as an ordinary application or as an OLE applet, just like DrawPlus and PhotoPlus. See the section on DrawPlus for more information about ordinary applications and OLE applets.

In the TablePlus work screen (Figure 17.5), the preview window contains the worksheet. The rows and columns are labeled with numbers and letters, respectively. The highlighted cell is the selected cell; text in this cell can be edited. You can select other cells by clicking on them with the mouse, or you can select ranges of cells by dragging it. You can also select whole rows and columns by clicking on the buttons labeling the row or columns, such as A or 1.

Experiment using the worksheet in the preview window. The hint line gives you a description of the different elements in the window.

As in DrawPlus and PhotoPlus, the front panel contains all the controls you need for formatting text in the selected range of cells. You can change the font, point size, style, alignment, and rotation angle of the text. And you can add formulas to the table and apply formatting to numbers (such as a currency format).

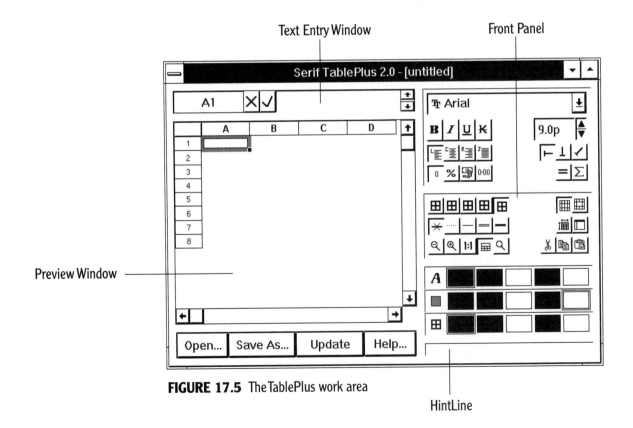

FIGURE 17.5 The TablePlus work area

The middle group of controls on the front panel lets you add lines to the table, join cells, alter the zoom level, use the Windows clipboard, and more.

The bottom group of controls lets you change the color of text, cells, backgrounds, and lines in the table. Again, refer to the hint line to find out what each button does.

The text entry window lets you type text in TablePlus. Anything you type goes into the currently selected cell as new text. If you click on the text entry window, you can edit any text that's already in the selected cell.

Quick Format

The Quick Format feature lets you automatically apply a style to your table. TablePlus comes with more than a dozen styles, that you can use or modify as needed. When you click on the Quick Format button, it brings up a dialog that gives you a list of formats and a preview window that shows you what they look like. When you click on the Options button, you'll see more buttons, which are used to set the specific parts of the table that the selected style is to affect. See Figure 17.6.

You can also define your own styles by creating a table and placing the file in the template directory.

Quick Fill

When tables have a regular sequence of text entries—for example, numbers from 1 to 10 or months from January to December—you can use the Quick Fill feature to enter the sequence automatically. To do so, follow these steps:

1. Select the cell where the sequence will start.

2. Type in whatever you want for the start of the sequence, such as 1 or January.

3. Click on the little square in the lower-right corner of the selected cell.

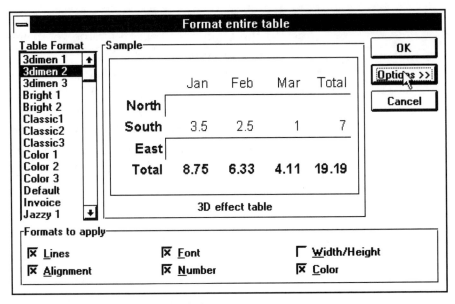

FIGURE 17.6 The Quick Format dialog

4. Drag that handle down to cover the rest of the cells that will be in the sequence. When you release the mouse button, the sequence should be complete.

TypePlus

TypePlus is a PagePlus add-on that lets you take small bits of text and apply special effects to them. Text that's been spiffed up with special effects is great for creating logos, headlines, and any other snazzy effect you need for your desktop publishing creations. TypePlus is as simple to use as entering type (or pasting it in from the clipboard) and then clicking on the buttons in TypePlus to apply a range of effects. You can arrange type on an arc, a circle, a button, or a Bezier curve. Additional graphics tools let you create effects for backgrounds or import pictures for use as a background or a special effect.

Installing TypePlus

To run TypePlus you need at least a 286 system with 2 MB of RAM, running Windows in standard mode. Serif recommends, however, that you have a 386SX or better with at least 3 MB of RAM, running Windows in enhanced mode. TypePlus takes up about 1 MB of space on your hard drive.

As with other PagePlus add-ons, you can use TypePlus as an ordinary application or as an OLE applet. See the section on DrawPlus regarding the differences between the two.

Using TypePlus

The tabs bar in the upper-left corner is used for selecting the current layer in TypePlus. To change the layer you're working on, select it by clicking on the tab for that layer. When you select a layer, the other layers are shown in the preview window at a lower intensity. When you add a new layer to your document, TypePlus creates a new tab on the tabs bar. Each tab has a graphic on it to show what type of layer it represents (for example, a text layer has an A on it).

The text entry window is where you enter and edit text. You can only enter text if the current layer is a text layer. See Figure 17.7.

The preview window in TypePlus shows you what the final document will look like. The inner dotted rectangle shows the area that will be exported when you paste the object into the final document. This inner rectangle is known as the clipping area. If you click on the preview window, it refreshes the display and shows the latest version of the document.

The front panel includes controls for creating, modifying, sizing, and moving layers. The top row of buttons are for creating and deleting layers.

The next level includes the Layer Modification buttons. These are like the change bar in PagePlus in that they change according to what type of operation you are performing. The third level down contains the Outline Width/Shadow buttons. Here you can change outlines, shadows, and the size of the document.

At the bottom are buttons for controlling colors in outlines, fills, and shadows.

Text Entry   Preview Window   Front Panel

TabsBar

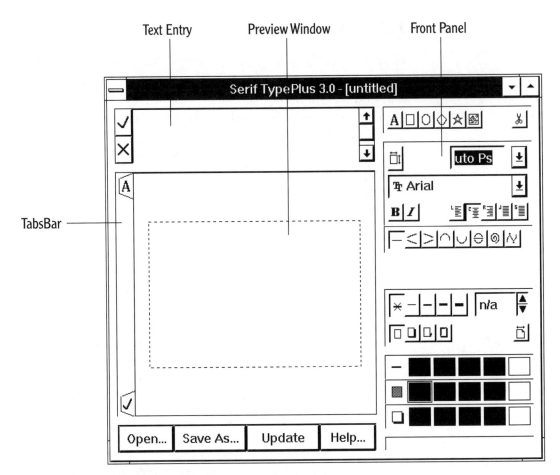

FIGURE 17.7 The TypePlus work screen

Go ahead and experiment with TypePlus. Use the hint line to see what the buttons do.

APPENDICES

Glossary

B

Bandwidth. Bandwidth is the measurement of the signal transmitted to the computer's monitor, in MHz.

Bit map. A set of dots (bits) that makes up a graphic image.

Bleed. A graphics term meaning when a photo or other image runs off the page.

Blueline. A printed proof made from the negative that will be used to create printing plates.

C

Camera-ready. A document that is in final form, ready to be shot by a professional printer.

Caption. Text that explains a photograph or illustration.

CD-ROM (compact disc–read-only memory). An optical storage disk that stores 750 MB of data.

Central processing unit (CPU). A computer's internal storage, processing, and control circuitry. It contains the arithmetic logic unit (ALU), control unit, and primary storage. The ALU and control unit reside on the microprocessor chip.

Characters per second (CPS). A measure of printer speed.

Clip art. Pictures and graphics in electronic format, either on CD or floppy disk, that can be used in a desktop publishing document.

CMYK. The four colors—cyan, magenta, yellow, and black—that make up a process color image.

Color separation. The process of breaking out the four colors used in continuous-tone color artwork (cyan, magenta, yellow, and black) for reproduction by a commercial printer.

Columns. Vertical blocks of text in a document.

Commercial printer. A printing company that prints business cards, brochures, newspapers, and more, usually using offset lithography.

Complex instruction set computer (CISC). A computer whose CPU responds to a relatively large set of instructions, as compared to RISC. Pentium systems use RISC technology.

Crop marks. Symbols that are placed in the margin outside a page to indicate the area to be printed and/or trimmed.

Crosshair. The cursor, which looks like a cross, that appears in PagePlus when you are drawing a box on-screen.

D

Deck. Part of a newspaper story. The deck sits between the headline and the main text and gives more information about the story.

Disk Operating System (DOS). The software that contains the basic set of instructions that runs an IBM PC or compatible.

Drop cap. Large initial letters that extend below the body of text.

Dots per inch (DPI). A measurement of the density of dots in a printed document or on-screen. Three hundred DPI equals 300 dots per square inch.

E

ELF (extremely low frequency). A magnetic field generated by computer monitors and other electrical devices.

Emboss. To add a design or text on top of another layer.

Enhanced mode. An operating system option. By using the virtual memory capabilities of the 386 processor, programs can use more memory than what appears to be physically available. Enhanced mode is essential for multitasking.

Environmental Protection Agency (EPA). An agency of the U.S. government.

Extended Architecture (XA). An architecture used in CD-ROM drives that transfer data at high speeds.

F

Font. A set of characters of the same typeface, style, weight, and size. In PagePlus and other software applications, font refers only to typeface. There are separate controls for size, style, and weight.

Footer. Text that runs along the bottom of a publication, is repeated on each page, and usually contains information such as the chapter number, date, or page number.

For Position Only (FPO). A label used on camera-ready documents to indicate where final art should be placed.

G

Gamma correction. A mathematical function that adjusts the midtones of an image based on a curve rather than on a linear change in brightness or darkness.

General protection fault (GPF). An error message that tells you that Windows has crashed.

Graphical user interface (GUI). An interface that runs over the operating system and lets you select menu items using a mouse or other input device.

Grayscale. A series of shades from black to white used in computer graphics.

Gutter. The space between two facing pages.

Header. Text that runs across the top of a publication, usually indicating the title or chapter.

Headline. The title of a document, publication, chapter, or story.

I-beam. The cursor, which looks like an I, that appears in PagePlus when you're inputting text.

Integrated drive electronics (IDE). A common type of hard disk drive architecture in which the electronics are on the drive rather than on the controller. (Compare to Small Computer System Interface SCSI.)

Justified. Describes lines of type that are exactly the same length, such that right and left margins align. Type can be right- and/or left-justified.

Kilohertz (kHz). A measurement of the number of lines displayed on a monitor in a one-second period.

L

Landscape. A horizontal page orientation, in which the page is wide rather than tall.

M

Megabyte (MB). A unit of measurement equal to approximately one million bytes.

Megahertz (MHz). A measurement of the speed at which the signal is transmitted to the computer monitor.

Moire. A pattern created when printing process colors, caused by the overlapping of screens.

Motherboard. A slotted board that resides inside a microcomputer, upon which other boards that contain the basic circuitry for a computer or computer component can be mounted.

MPR II. Also called Swedac. A set of guidelines developed by the Swedish government for the maximum emissions of very low frequency (VLF) and extremely low frequency (ELF) magnetic and electric fields.

Multitasking. Running several applications at the same time.

N

Noninterlaced. A method of scanning an image on a monitor. A noninterlaced monitor draws every consecutive line, rather than every second line as in an interlaced display. Noninterlaced scanning requires a monitor with sufficient bandwidth to handle the graphics signal, but it results in a steady, nonflickering image.

O

OCR (optical character recognition). The machine recognition of printed or typed text.

Offset printing. Printing, done commonly by commercial printers, using offset lithography.

Operating system. The software layer that controls the computer hardware and acts as the interface between the hardware and the applications.

OPI (open prepress interface). A prepress standard specification.

P

Page description language (PDL). The language computers and printers use to communicate.

Pages per minute (PPM). A standard by which printer speed is measured.

Pantone. A patented process for matching colors. Pantone Matching System (PMS) colors can be specified from a swatch book and then duplicated by a commercial printer.

Photo CD. A graphics standard, set by Kodak, for photographs stored on compact disc.

Pixels (picture elements). The individual dots on the monitor that make up an image. A standard VGA screen of 640 by 480 resolution has 307,200 pixels on screen.

Pixelize. A process that makes a picture almost unrecognizable by replacing square groups of pixels with pixels of the average color of all the pixels in the group.

Portrait. A page orientation in which the page is placed vertically, or is tall rather than wide.

Posterize. Making a photograph look as if the picture were painted on a poster, with a smaller number of colors rather than in full color.

PostScript. A standard graphics page description language developed by Adobe. It lets you scale a variety of fonts and produce high-quality text.

Process color. A system for printing all visible colors from cyan, magenta, yellow, and black (CMYK).

Property. The value of an object, such as color or font.

Pull quotes. Also called breakouts, callouts, or blurbs. Pull quotes serve as both an informational and a graphical element.

R

Ragged. Describes lines of text that end at irregular intervals. Also called unjustified.

Random-access memory (RAM). Computer memory that stores data while the computer is in use. When the computer is turned off, data in RAM is destroyed.

Randomizing. Creating a pop-art effect in which each color in a graphic is changed to another color—randomly.

Reduced instruction set computer (RISC). A computer whose CPU responds to a relatively small set of computer instructions, as compared to CISC. RISC CPUs are faster than CISC because of the smaller set of instructions that they use.

Refresh rate. The number of times per second a screen image is redrawn on-screen.

Register. The alignment of the printer's plates when printing colors. Registration marks are commonly applied to pages that include four-color separations.

RGB. The colors red, green, and blue, which are used to form the colors on computer monitors.

S

Scanner. A hardware device that converts photographs or other printed material into a bitmapped graphics file.

Service bureau. A company that provides high-resolution output of your desktop publishing files.

Single in-line memory modules (SIMMS). A module you plug into your computer's motherboard that lets you add RAM (memory).

Small computer system interface (SCSI). Pronounced "scuzzy," this standard computer interface port connects up to seven peripherals, such as drives, scanners, and printers.

Smoothing. The process of reducing the number of small, isolated, single-color areas in a graphic.

Snapping. The process of moving text and graphics into place according to a ruler guide. This can be done automatically by turning a "snapping" function on.

Solarizing. The process of distorting a photo by inverting its brightest parts.

Spot color. Color that doesn't use the four process colors, but which consists instead of solid-color type and design elements.

Stripping. Prepress work that includes the assembling of negatives or positives to create a printing plate for a page.

Style sheet. A library of styles you've selected for a given publication. A style sheet can be used for all your publications.

Subhead. Text heading used to introduce a new section of a story. Subheads guide the reader to specific information in a story.

Super VGA. An enhancement of the VGA standard, capable of displaying between 800 lines horizontally by 600 lines vertically, and 1,024 lines horizontally by 768 lines vertically, with 16 or 256 colors simultaneously displayed.

Swap space. Files that are hidden on a hard disk. Software uses this space to swap information from memory to the drive, as a temporary storage device.

Swedac. See MPR II.

T

Thumbnail. Proofs of the pages of a document in a reduced size, so you can see multiple pages at a glance on one proof sheet.

Trapping. Lines that appear when one printed color touches another.

TSR (Terminate and Stay Resident). A program that remains in system RAM so you will always have access to it.

TWAIN. A driver standard that ensures that scanners work with optical character recognition (OCR) software and other Windows applications.

Typeface. A family of fonts; for example, Arial or Helvetica.

V

Video Electronics Standards Association (VESA). A standards organization for the video industry.

Video graphics adapter (VGA). A video image with a pixel resolution of 640 by 480.

VLF (very low frequency). A magnetic field generated by computer monitors and other electrical devices.

W

White space. The space on a page that is not consumed by text or graphics.

WYSIWYG ("What you see is what you get"). A term used to describe software that shows the same image on-screen that you will get on paper. Pronounced "wizzy-wig."

Acronyms and Abbreviations

CD-ROM—compact disc, read-only memory

CMYK—cyan, magenta, yellow, and black

CISC—complex instruction set computer

CPS—characters per second

CPU—central processing unit

DOS—disk operating system

DPI—dots per inch

ELF—extremely low frequency

EPA—Environmental Protection Agency

FPO—for position only

GPF—general protection fault

GUI—graphical user interface

IDE—integrated drive electronics

kHz—kilohertz

MB—megabytes

MHz—megahertz

OCR—optical character recognition

OPI—Open Prepress Interface

PDL—page description language

PMS—Pantone Matching System

PPM—pages per minute

RAM—random access memory

RISC—reduced instruction set computer

SCSI—small computer system interface

SIMMS—single in-line memory modules

SVGA—super video graphics adapter

TSR—terminate and stay resident

VESA—Video Electronics Standards Association

VGA—video graphics adapter

VLF—very low frequency

WYSIWYG—what you see is what you get

XA—extended architecture

Resource Guide

The following resource guide includes a small sampling of the manufacturers of the products described in Chapter 1 as well as in other sections of the book. This resource guide is not intended to make specific product or vendor recommendations, but is designed to assist you in finding products to outfit your desktop publishing office.

Hardware

Systems

Acer America
800-733-2237

Alaris
510-770-5700

ALR
800-444-4257
714-581-6770

AST Research
800-876-4278

AT&T Global Information Solutions
800-509-9609

Austin Computer Systems
800-752-1577

Compaq Computer
800-345-1518

Dell Computer
800-289-3355

Gateway 2000
800-846-2000
605-232-2000

Hewlett-Packard
800-752-0900
408-553-2922

IBM
800-426-7735

Micron Computer, Inc.
800-669-6744

NEC Technologies
800-632-4636

Toshiba
800-457-7777

Packard Bell
800-733-4411

Zeos International Ltd.
800-554-5220

Texas Instruments
800-848-3927

CD-ROM Drives

Chinon America
800-441-0222
310-533-0274

Plextor
800-886-3935
408-980-1838

Hitachi Home Electronics
800-369-0422
310-537-8383

Sony Electronics
800-352-7669
408-432-0190

MediaTECH
800-860-9433

Storage Devices
714-562-5500

Micro Solutions
800-890-7227
815-756-3411

Teac
800-888-4923
213-726-0303

NEC Technologies
800-388-8888
708-860-9500

Toshiba America
Information Systems, Disk
Division
714-455-0407

Pioneer New Media
Technologies, Inc.
800-444-6784
408-988-1702

Monitors

Altima
800-356-9990
510-356-5600

MAG InnoVision
800-827-3998
714-751-2008

Nanao USA Corp.
800-800-5202
310-325-5202

NEC
800-388-8888
708-860-9500

Optiquest, Inc.
909-468-3750

Panasonic
800-742-8086

Philips
800-835-3506

Sampo
404-449-6220

Sceptre
800-788-2878
714-993-9193

Sigma Designs, Inc.
800-845-8086

Sony
800-352-7669

SuperMac
(E-Machines)
800-334-3005

ViewSonic
800-888-8583

WEN Technology Corp.
914-347-4100

Mice

Appoint
800-448-1184
510-463-3003

Kensington
800-535-4242

Logitech
510-795-8500

Microsoft Corp.
800-426-9400

MicroSpeed
800-438-7733
510-490-1665

Prohance Technologies
415-967-5774

Mouse Systems Corp.
800-886-6423
510-656-1117

Keyboards

Integrated Technology
800-393-8889

Key Tronic Corp.
800-262-6006
509-928-8000

Kinesis Corp
206-455-9220

Lexmark
800-426-2468

Chicony America
714-630-6662

Scanners

AVR Technology
800-544-6243
408-434-1115

Hewlett-Packard
800-722-6538

Microtek Lab
800-654-4160
310-297-5000

Calera Recognition Systems
800-442-5372

Canon Computer Systems
800-848-4123
714-438-3000

Mustek, Inc.
800-468-7835
714-453-0110

Epson America
800-289-3776
310-782-0770

Umax Technologies
800-562-0311
510-651-8883

Printers

Alps America
800-825-2577
408-432-6000

Brother International
Corp.
800-276-7746
908-356-8880

C-Tech Electronics, Inc.
800-347-4017
714-833-1165

DataProducts Corp.
800-334-3174
818-887-8000

Epson America, Inc.
800-289-3776
310-782-0770

GCC Technologies, Inc.
800-942-3233
617-275-5800

Hewlett-Packard
800-752-0900

Mannesmann Tally Corp.
800-843-1347
206-251-5500

Mitsubishi International
Corporation
914-997-4999
415-496-5447

NEC Technologies, Inc.
800-632-4636

Okidata
800-654-3282
609-235-2600

Panasonic
Communications
800-742-8086
201-348-7000

QMS, Inc.
800-523-2696
205-633-4300

Sharp Electronics Corp.
800-237-4277

Star Micronics, Inc.
800-447-4700

Tektronix
800-835-6100

Xerox
800-832-6979

Software

Clip Art

Acuris
800-652-8747
415-329-1920

Allegro New Media
800-424-1992
201-808-1992

Arro International
201-746-9620

Artbeats
800-444-9392
503-863-4429

Autodesk
800-879-4233
415-332-2344

Bruce Jones Design
800-843-3873
617-350-6166

Cartesia Software
800-334-4291
609-397-1611

CE Technology
800-654-1138
818-981-4121

Design Plus
800-231-3461
212-645-2686

**Innovative Advertising &
Design**
800-255-0562
802-879-1164

Olduvai
800-548-5151
305-670-1112

Ray Dream
800-846-0111
415-960-0768

Sense Interactive
800-757-3673
713-523-5757

Serif, Inc.
603-889-8650

Studio Advertising Art
702-641-7041

Desktop Publishing Software

Adobe
800-628-2320

NEBS
800-882-5254

Corel/Ventura Software
800-722-6735

Quark
800-788-7835

Frame
800-843-7263

Serif, Inc.
603-889-8650

Interleaf
800-955-5323

Softkey International
617-494-1200

Microsoft Corporation
800-426-9400

Wizard Works, Inc.
(612) 559-5140

Drawing Software

Adobe
800-833-6687

Micrografx
800-733-3729
214-234-1769

Aldus
800-333-2538
206-628-2320

Serif, Inc.
603-889-8650

Corel, Inc.
800-772-6735
613-728-8200

Photo CDs

Allegro New Media
800-424-1992
201-808-1992

CMCD
800-664-2623
415-703-9900

Creative Resources
800-358-2278
510-843-3408

D'Pix
800-238-3749
614-299-7192

Form and Function
415-664-4010

Image Club Graphics
800-661-9410
403-262-8008

Knowledge Media
800-782-3766
916-872-7487

PhotoDisc
800-528-3472
206-441-9355

Sense Interactive
800-757-3673
713-523-5757

Texture City
310-836-9224

Work for Hire
914-769-3776

Photo Editing and Special Effects

Adobe Systems
800-628-2320

Altamira Software
800-425-8264
415-332-5801

Claris
800-252-2747
408-727-8227

Computer Associates
800-225-5224
516-342-5224

Corel
800-772-6735

Deneba
800-733-6322
305-596-5644

Fauve Software
800-898-2787
919-380-9933

Fractal Design
800-297-2665
408-688-5300

ImageWare
619-673-8600

Innovative Data Design
510-680-6818

Micrografx
800-733-3729
214-234-1769

Pacific Gold Coast
800-732-3002
516-759-3011

Pixel Resources
800-851-1427
404-449-4947

Ron Scott
713-529-5868

Serif, Inc.
603-889-8650

SoftKey
800-227-5609
404-428-0008

Specular International
800-433-7732

Screen Capture Programs

Baseline Publishing
901-682-9676

Inset Systems
203-740-2400

DeltaPoint
408-648-4000

LEAD Technologies
704-549-5532

Halcyon Software
408-378-9898

Mainstay
805-484-9400

Inner Media
800-962-2949
603-465-3216

North Coast Software
603-664-6000

Upgrading to PagePlus 3.0 and Other Serif Products

Serif's PagePlus offers a tremendous amount of computing power for the price. With PagePlus add-on products, the beginning desktop publisher can grow into the product and explore many avenues. The following is a brief description of each of Serif's desktop publishing products.

Serif Products

PagePlus—A basic desktop publishing program that combines ease of use and power.

TypePlus—A text effects applet that lets you create text effects and logos. TypePlus is an OLE applet, so it works with any Windows application.

TablePlus—A powerful minispreadsheet that lets you create tables, invoices, price lists, and more. TablePlus is an OLE applet, so it works with any Windows application.

DrawPlus—This vector drawing program lets you create illustrations, modify and recolor clip art images, distort type, and more. DrawPlus is an OLE applet, so it works with any Windows application.

PhotoPlus—This photo editing applet lets you adjust color, brightness, and contrast and apply filter effects to scanned photos, from PhotoPacks, and other bitmapped images.

ArtPacks—Each Serif ArtPack contains over five hundred professionally drawn images, in both black and white and color. These fully scalable vector graphics are Windows metafiles and can therefore be imported to other Windows applications as well.

FontPacks—Serif FontPacks each contain over one hundred classic and decorative TrueType fonts. TrueType fonts can be used with any Windows 3.1 (or higher) application.

PhotoPacks—Serif PhotoPacks each contain one hundred full-color images in Kodak Photo CD format. These photos are royalty-free and ready for color separation.

PagePlus Publishing Suite—This CD-ROM contains all the above applications and resource packs. Armed with the Serif Publishing Suite, you can integrate word processing, drawings and illustrations, tables, text effects, fonts, clip art, and photos into your desktop publishing creations.

Upgrading

The CD enclosed with your starter kit includes PagePlus Intro, DrawPlus Intro, and a collection of ArtPack clip art. PagePlus Intro is not the same as the Introductory level in PagePlus 3.0, which we use in the lessons in Chapters 6 through 9. The copy of PagePlus 3.0 included on the CD is available for use on a time-limited basis and will work for only sixty days after you have installed the product. In addition, this version can only be installed once.

If you are interested in using PagePlus for an unlimited time, refer to the registration message on the CD, which gives you a number to call (with your credit card number), to receive your registration and unlocking number.

PagePlus 3.0 regularly sells for $99; however, to unlock it from the version enclosed on your CD, Serif is offering a 60 percent discount. You can register and unlock PagePlus 3.0 for $39.

In addition, if you want to get the full Serif Publishing suite, which includes PagePlus 3.0, TypePlus, DrawPlus, TablePlus, PhotoPlus, and additional clip art from ArtPacks and FontPacks, Serif is offering a 60 percent discount to users of the enclosed CD. This software comes on a CD and regularly sells for $100. It is discounted for readers of this book to $59 plus $6 shipping. To take advantage of this offer, a telephone number for ordering information is included in the registration message on the CD.

How to Choose the Right DTP Software

Desktop publishing software runs the gamut from word processing packages that have desktop publishing capabilities to high-end electronic publishing packages that are used for huge manuals that may be thousands of pages long. How do you choose from this wide range of options? If you stick with those products that fall into the Windows-based desktop publishing category, you'll limit the field to about ten products.

Within those ten products, prices range from a low of $49.99 for CompuWorks Publisher all the way up to $995 for Interleaf 6. The difference in the two products is monumental. A desktop publisher who could use CompuWorks Publisher would have no need of the power of an Interleaf, and conversely, an Interleaf user would find CompuWorks Publisher seriously inadequate. So, how do you choose? You begin with knowing your needs, and then you find the product that meets them.

The chart here shows some of the features found in each of the ten desktop publishing products. There are some commonalities among the less expensive packages and those at the high end. It's natural to want to divide those ten into two categories: low-end and high-end, but it's not that simple, because many of the lower-priced packages offer some of the same sophisticated features of the higher-priced packages. As far as features go, there is much overlap. But features are not everything. Some of the high-end packages offer powerful features, but to use them, you have to know all kinds of ridiculous codes and tag your text in very specific ways. Additionally, just because a product lacks a particular feature does not mean that it is any less sophisticated than another. The pasteboard metaphor, for example, is one feature that not all users want, nor is it one that all packages offer. There are other features, even in the most expensive packages, that are not used, or needed, by everyone.

COMPARISON OF TEN DESKTOP-PUBLISHING PACKAGES

Product name, version	CompuWorks Publisher 1.0	Corel Ventura 5	FrameMaker 5.0	Interleaf 6.1
Company	WizardWorks	Corel	Frame Technology	Interleaf
Price	$49.99	$495 CD only; $595 CD and cassette	$895	$995
Text wrap	yes	yes	yes	yes
Adobe Type 1 or TrueType fonts	yes	yes	yes	yes
Word processor	no	yes	yes	yes
Auto. text flow to multiple columns	yes	yes	yes	yes
Text flow to noncontiguous pages	yes	yes	yes	no
Custom page sizes	no	yes	yes	yes
Pasteboard metaphor	no	yes	no	no
Thumbnails	no	no	yes	yes
Defined styles	no	yes	yes	yes
Color matching	no	yes	yes	no
Table editor	no	yes	yes	yes
Support for Pantone palette	no	yes	yes	no
Color separation	no	yes	yes	no
Multiuser access	no	yes	yes	yes
Hypertext links	no	yes	yes	yes
DDE	no	yes	yes	no
OLE 2	no	yes	no	yes
Photo CD	no	yes	no	no
TWAIN	no	yes	no	no
Cross-platform compatability	no	no	yes	yes

*PageMagic lets you import files from other platforms.

**PageMaker allows text flow to noncontiguous pages through templates.

Page Magic	PageMaker 5.0	PagePlus 3.0	PFS: Publisher 1.1	Publisher	QuarkXPress 3.31
NEBS	Adobe	Serif	Softkey	Microsoft	Quark
$67.95	$895	$99	$119.95	$99.95	$895
yes	yes	yes	yes	yes	yes
yes	yes	yes	yes	yes	yes
yes	yes	yes	yes	yes	yes
yes	yes	yes	no	yes	yes
yes	no**	yes	yes	yes	yes
yes	yes	yes	yes	yes	yes
no	yes	yes	no	yes	yes
no	yes	yes	yes	no	yes
yes	yes	yes	yes	yes	yes
no	yes	yes	no	no	yes
no	yes	no	no	yes	no
no	yes	yes	no	no	yes
no	yes	yes	no	no	yes
no	yes	yes	no	no	no
no	no	no	no	no	no
no	yes	yes	no	no	no
yes	yes	no	yes	yes	no
yes	yes	yes	no	yes	yes
no	yes	yes	no	yes	no
yes*	yes	no	no	no	yes

The chart on pages 242–243 is meant to help you find the desktop publishing package that's best for you. You'll see that many of the packages have features in common, but differ greatly in price. In many cases you'll want to take a look at the software to find the one that has the easiest interface for you to use.

When using this chart, be aware that the prices are suggested retail prices at the time of publication. Likewise, the version numbers are the most current at the time of publication. Version numbers, features, and prices are all subject to change, but this features list gives you a quick way to see the differences in today's lineup of desktop publishing software.

Entry-level Software

While it's difficult to categorize specific packages as low end or high end, it's clear from the chart that there is a huge price difference. We'll call the least expensive products entry-level software, because they are generally easy to use and are designed for beginning desktop publishers. Generally, the programs do not have the typographical, layout, and color functions found in more expensive packages, although this is not true across the board. What they do have is basic cut, copy, and paste functions along with import filters and the ability to handle Adobe and TrueType fonts. Some of the entry-level packages are easier to use than others. Publisher, for example, has Wizards, which are supposed to make document creation almost automatic.

Operating Systems

The term "cross-platform compatibility" on the chart refers to the ability to run the software under Windows, for example, while using files prepared on a Macintosh. Only desktop publishing packages that have versions for other operating systems can offer true cross-platform compatibility. Of these ten, all run under Windows,

FrameMaker runs on the Mac and PowerMac as well as under UNIX, Interleaf also runs under UNIX, PageMaker also runs on the Mac, Publisher also runs under OS/2, and QuarkXPress also runs on the Mac.

Like the pasteboard metaphor, this is a feature that not all users will need. But for those who do, it is a crucial one. While manufacturers can claim that their software will cross from Windows to Mac to UNIX to OS/2, it's best to run a test before buying a particular product. Some fare better than others in this realm.

Color

The ability to match colors and to color separate is one area that sets the entry-level software apart from the rest. Serif's PagePlus is an exception to this rule, because it offers sophisticated color capabilities for a comparatively low price. QuarkXPress is known for its EfiColor QuarkXTension, which is an unrivaled system that matches monitor colors with colors from output devices—giving new meaning to the term What You See Is What You Get.

Add-ons

While many desktop publishing packages offer all the capabilities that most users need, others have add-on packages to meet individual demands. Be careful about getting too excited about add-ons, however. Some desktop publishing manufacturers offer add-ons for functions that really should have been included in the product in the first place. Other manufacturers have add-ons that accomplish very specific tasks, sometimes even targeted to users in a particular industry. Add-ons, by the way, are not all developed by the manufacturer of the desktop publishing software. If you need something very specific, find out if it's available from a third party.

Corel Ventura, for example, offers additional utilities for font kerning, database publishing, image editing, screen capture, database querying, and more. PageMaker offers more than fifty add-ons. Serif's

Publishing Suite adds TablePlus, TypePlus, DrawPlus, and PhotoPlus to PagePlus. Publisher offers three Design Packs that add templates, fonts, and clip art. And to QuarkXpress, users can add more than 100 "Xtensions."

The High End and Beyond

For users who go beyond the needs of traditional desktop publishing packages, there's document publishing. When documents run into thousands of pages and involve input from multiple people, departments, and computer systems, you need advanced document processing software that supports multiple operating systems, a variety of output media, different programming language interfaces, multiple security levels, and more. For example, an industry that stores graphics, text, database, and spreadsheet documents in different formats at various locations may want to pull them all under one umbrella to be distributed in any format that's necessary. FrameMaker and Interleaf are in the document processing realm, although they also have features in common with the high-end desktop publishing applications.

Desktop publishers who demand speed and performance from software will be running the latest 32-bit platforms and will want to stick with software that's designed for 32-bit systems. Many manufacturers of high-end desktop publishing software will be releasing Windows NT and Windows95 versions in the near future. If your work puts you in the power publishing realm, stay tuned. If not, the software listed here should meet your needs.

A Quick Look at PagePlus Intro

While the lessons in this book are based on PagePlus 3.0, you get to use it for just 60 days before you have to call to unlock your own registered version. PagePlus Intro, on the other hand, is yours to keep and use indefinitely.

PagePlus Intro is similar to version 3.0, but is actually a very different product. You can use Intro to create simple projects such as ads, invitations, business letterhead, and more. The following is a quick rundown on how to use PagePlus Intro, used by permission of Serif, Inc.

Starting PagePlus Intro

Start PagePlus Intro now by double-clicking on the PagePlus Intro icon that can be found in the Serif Applications group.

While PagePlus Intro is loading it displays a window containing the Serif Tiger. If PagePlus Intro won't start at all (doesn't display the Tiger), fails part way through starting, or is otherwise unreliable, refer to the Troubleshooting: Machine Setup topic of the Install help file.

After a few seconds, PagePlus Intro displays its initial working screen, then immediately calls up a Registration window on top of the working screen. Now is a great time to take a couple of minutes to call and register your copy of PagePlus Intro. If you prefer not to register now, click the button marked Done.

The registration screen will appear whenever the program is started/closed until you register your copy of PagePlus Intro. After you have cleared the Registration window, PagePlus Intro displays a "Welcome" screen. The Welcome screen is automatically displayed only the first time you start PagePlus Intro.

Please read the Welcome. This is where you'll find any late-breaking news. It also includes important License Agreement information which you should read right now. Welcome is a Help Topic, so once you've read it, close it by selecting File/Exit. If you ever want to read the Welcome screen again after this initial display, select Help/ Welcome.

After you've exited the Welcome, you will see the PagePlus Intro Working Screen.

The PagePlus Intro Working Screen

Now you can see the normal working screen. It's simply a blank page on the pasteboard, ready for you to place text and graphics.

As you can see, PagePlus Intro has a title bar, menus, and scroll bars just like your other Windows programs. It also has a ToolBar, Page and Pasteboard areas, Rulers, and HintLine.

THE TOOLBAR

The ToolBar contains tool icons that you select in order to create and manipulate objects. From left to right:

- Pointer (for selecting, sizing, and moving objects)

- Text (for creating free text and editing any text)

- Frame (for creating frames containing columns for text to flow into)

- Line, Straight Line, Box, Rounded Box, Oval (all for creating graphic objects)

- Rotate (to rotate text, graphics, and pictures to 45-degree angles)

- Zoom (to change the view size to view at any percentage size)

- Import Art (click to import Art & Border files from Serif Art-Packs or double-click to import pictures in any image format)

- TypePlus (to import work from Serif's TypePlus applet—if installed)

- TableEdit (to import work from Serif's TableEdit applet—if installed)

THE PAGE AND PASTEBOARD

Most of the PagePlus Intro display is taken up by the page (artwork) area and a surrounding "pasteboard" area.

The page area (displayed as a shadowed box) is where you put page layout guides and the text, graphics, and pictures that you want to print. The pasteboard area is where you generally keep any text, graphics, or pictures that are being prepared or waiting to be positioned on the page area.

This page and pasteboard arrangement is very convenient. In fact, it is an electronic equivalent of the system used by traditional graphic designers: they kept bits of text and graphics on a large pasteboard, and then carefully pasted final arrangements of text and graphics onto a page-sized artwork sheet pinned down in the middle of the board.

RULERS

The rulers run along the top and left of your window and provide a visual way to position, size, and move objects on your page. You can control the basic ruler units using Options/Preferences. Move the rulers by dragging and double-clicking on their intersection. Create guides on your page by clicking on the rulers. Guides are non-printing lines that are used to help you line things up. The ruler divisions and any guides you have create a grid to which objects can be snapped, if snapping is switched on (Page/Snapping).

THE HINTLINE

To make it easy for you to learn the program, PagePlus Intro provides feedback in the HintLine as you move the mouse over iconic areas of the screen.

Watch the HintLine as you move the mouse over the buttons of the ToolBar to find out which button does what.

The HintLine can make an enormous difference in how easy it is to learn and use PagePlus—but only if you remember to watch it!

Creating a Test Page

To introduce you to working with PagePlus Intro and to ensure that PagePlus Intro is correctly installed and working on your system, we'll create and print a very simple test page.

DRAW A BOX

1. Move the mouse pointer over the ToolBar, to the sixth button of the row (it has a box on its face).

2. Click the left mouse button and move the mouse into the middle of the page.

3. Drag out a box shape (click and hold down the left button, move diagonally, then release the button).

A box appears where you have drawn it, with a set of default properties.

The ToolBar also changes, allowing you direct access to functions for changing the look of the created object. Try clicking on the five buttons (with horizontal line icons) that have appeared, grouped together to the right of the ToolBar, and see how the outline of the box changes.

Now for some text . . .

TYPE SOME TEXT

1. Move the mouse pointer of the ToolBar, to the second button on the row (it has an A on its face).

2. Now click the left mouse button and move the mouse over the page somewhere.

3. Click the left mouse button—a blinking caret (text edit cursor) is displayed on the page.

4. Type in a few words. The text appears with a default set of properties. . . which means you can't read it in the current fit-page-in-window view.

Simply select the Zoom tool and drag, surrounding the text you just typed. Now you should be able to read your text. Remember, the

Zoom tool is great for enlarging the view so you can see specific areas of the page more clearly.

PRINT THE PAGE

1. Select File/Print.

2. Click on the OK button.

If the page doesn't come out OK, check your Windows and printer setup. Try printing from Paintbrush (supplied with Windows, located in the Accessories group). If Paintbrush won't print, take a close look at your Microsoft Windows Users Guide. Otherwise refer to the Troubleshooting: Printing topic in the on-line Help file.

WHAT NEXT?

You now have PagePlus Intro installed and running, have created and printed your first page, and know the basic layout for the PagePlus Intro working screen.

Following that comes a short PagePlus Intro Tutorial that guides you through the creation of the basic page design. After you have completed the tutorial, we suggest you take time to have a good look at the PagePlus Intro menus, and browse through the help topics that contain detailed references on all the menus, tools, and keyboard shortcuts for PagePlus Intro.

PagePlus Intro Tutorial

This 10-minute tutorial guides you through the creation of a simple one-page piece. The aim is to introduce you to a few more of the basics of using PagePlus Intro. After that, it's up to you to explore and learn by experimenting, looking at the HintLine, and by reading the on-line help.

STARTING THE PAGE

Start PagePlus Intro if necessary. If PagePlus Intro is already running, do a File/New (just say No if prompted to save). You're ready to start work.

Establish the basic page layout for this page. This is always the first step for any publication.

1. Select Page/Page Setup.

2. Make sure your page size matches your printer, set columns to 1, and click OK.

THE FOOTBALL PICTURE

Although you can add items to a PagePlus Intro publication in any order you like, typically you would start with the primary elements. In this case, that means either the picture or the three-column block of text. We'll do the football picture first.

Import the `Footbll2.WMF` picture (an ArtPack sample supplied with PagePlus Intro) using the Art & Borders feature of PagePlus Intro.

1. Click on the Art & Borders/Import Picture button on the ToolBar. PagePlus Intro displays the Art & Borders dialog.

2. Select ArtPack One Samples from the Category field at the bottom of the dialog.

3. Double-click on `Footbll2.WMF` in the files list. After a few moments, the cursor will change to a cross-hair with a box to indicate that the picture is ready to be put on your page.

4. Drag the mouse in a rectangle covering the top half of the page.

5. Release the mouse button—the picture is imported and placed where you dragged.

6. If you didn't manage to place the picture correctly or at the right size, use the Pointer tool to move and/or resize it now.

THE BOX AROUND THE PICTURE

Draw the box using the Box tool from the ToolBar.

1. Ensure Snapping is on (the Page/Snapping menu entry should be ticked) so that the box snaps to the margin guides.

2. Draw a box to come about halfway down the page and fitting the left, top, and right margins—the box snaps to exactly align with the margin guides. Currently the box is on top of the picture (because it was drawn last).

3. Select Edit/Arrange/Send to Back.

Next we need to change some properties of the box to make it look the way we want.

1. Set the line weight to 1 point by clicking on the Line = 1 pt shortcut button on the ToolBar.

2. Select Graphics/Fill/Color and choose Clear for the box.

3. Select Graphics/Line/Color and set the line color to Blue.

THE HEADLINE

Create the headline using the Text tool.

1. Just below the box you've just drawn, double-click with the Text tool. The Edit Text window pops up. If the Edit Text window doesn't pop up, you either don't have the Text tool selected, or PagePlus Intro didn't realize that you double-clicked. Try again.

2. Type in "The Football Experience," and press Enter. Then type "is it rushing you by?" and click on OK.

Use the ToolBar and menus to change the way the headline looks, until you're happy with it.

1. Use the Size combo-box to change the size of the headline.

2. Use the Font combo-box to change the typeface: try Arial.

3. Use the Bold shortcut button (to set the typeface to bold).

4. Use the Color property to change the text color to red.

5. Use the Align property to set the alignment to center.

That's how the headline is basically done. For now, we'll move on to the three-column block of body text.

THE BODY TEXT

The body text of this piece consists of one stream of text that flows through three columns in a small area of the page, so we need to add a frame to the page.

Create a frame just below the headline, spanning the page margins, using the Frame tool.

1. Draw the frame, spanning the margins. Just like the box, the frame snaps to the margin guides. The frame's margins and column setup need to be changed to the necessary three-column arrangement. Frame options can be conveniently set via Page/Frame Setup..., but we'll use the mouse this time.

2. Move the mouse over the left frame margin guide. The mouse should display as a white double-headed arrow. If it displays as black double-headed arrow, you don't have the mouse over a guide.

3. Drag the guide as far left as it will go. This reduces the left margin to zero.

4. Repeat for the right guide, this time dragging the guide to the right.

5. Set three columns by using Page/Frame Setup.../Columns and entering 3.

OK, the layout's now done. What about some text? Rather than type the text, we're going to import it.

Select the Import Text dialog and import `Sample.WRI` from the PagePlus Intro Samples directory.

1. Select File/Import Text... or double-click on the frame's link button. If File/Import Text... is grayed out, you do not have the frame selected. Click on the frame with the Pointer tool until it displays handles.

2. Make sure List Files of Type is set to Write (*.WRI).

3. Change to the Samples directory.

4. Make sure the formatting option is not checked.

5. Double-click on the `Sample.WRI` file. The text loads into the publication and is flowed into the three-column layout.

OK, that just leaves paragraph and character formatting. We can format the first block in the frame and then invoke the PagePlus Intro Update Story function to update the whole text stream to the same formatting.

Use the ToolBar and menus to change the way the first block in the frame looks, until you're happy with it. Then use the Update Story feature to update the other text blocks.

1. Use the size property to adjust the size (to around 10 pt.).

2. Use the Color property to change the text color to red.

3. Use the Align property to set the alignment to justify.

4. When you're happy with how the first text block looks, select Text/Update Story—PagePlus Intro updates the entire story to include your changes.

THE LINE (AT THE BOTTOM)

The final element is a line graphic used as a border to the page. Draw the line using the 45-Degree Line tool from the ToolBar.

1. Select one of the line tools from the ToolBar.

2. Ensure Snapping is still on (the Page/Snapping menu entry should be checked).

3. Draw (drag) a line from the point where the left and bottom page margins meet to where the right and bottom margins meet. The line snaps to align to the bottom margin.

Now we'll use a shortcut to get the line to match the box we drew earlier.

1. Select the box you drew.

2. Select Edit/Copy—this copies the object and its formatting onto the Windows clipboard.

3. Select the line you just drew.

4. Select the Edit/Paste Format. PagePlus Intro updates the line to look like the first box.

FINISHING UP

Given the vagueness of earlier instruction in regard to the vertical positioning of some of the objects you've created, you may want to adjust a few of the items. If the headline looks like it could be moved down a little, do it now.

1. Select the headline using the Pointer tool.

2. Start moving it by dragging. Press the SHIFT key to constrain movement to one direction, then move the Headline up and down until it looks right.

SAVING YOUR WORK

PagePlus Intro follows the standard Windows approach for file-saving, which means that, even though you may have been working on a publication for several hours, none of your work is stored until you use File/Save or File/Save As... and save your publication file.

Save your work now as a PagePlus Intro publication.

1. Select File/Save. As is standard for all Windows applications, if your current file has a name (shown in the applications Title Bar), selecting File/Save will simply save the file without further prompting (all that will seem to happen is that there is a pause while the PC is doing something). However, if your current file is Untitled and you select File/Save, the application pops up the Save As dialog instead.

2. Type a filename into the File Name box. You should type just 1–8 characters. You don't need to type in the extension. PagePlus Intro will add it for you as either PPP for a publication or PPT for a template. The extension is important as it's what controls whether PagePlus Intro will list the file when you later pop up the File Open dialog.

3. Click on OK.

PagePlus Intro also includes an Autosave feature that automatically saves a hidden backup of your work, every few minutes. Don't worry about this. It has no affect on your own file saving. But if you ever have a system failure, this PagePlus Intro fail-safe could save you hours of hard work.

PRINT

1. Select File/Print.

2. Click on OK.

PagePlus 3.0 Keyboard Shortcuts

Keyboarding

PagePlus allows several forms of keyboard shortcuts.

Special functions: PagePlus has several features that are accessed by holding down a special key while performing an operation. For example, if you hold down the SHIFT key while creating or sizing a box, the box will be constrained to a square. See the next section for a complete list of shortcuts.

Menus using the keyboard: Rather than using the mouse to click over menus, you can use ALT + CHARACTER, where character is the letter shown as underlined on the menu. For example, ALT + E followed by ALT + I would select the Edit/Insert Object... dialog from the menus.

Menu shortcuts: Certain commonly used menus have quick single-keystroke shortcuts. Menu entries that have a shortcut will have CTRL + CHARACTER on their right, where CHARACTER is the letter to be pressed simultaneously with CONTROL to perform the menu operation. For example, CONTROL + S will do the File/Save operation.

Character access shortcuts: Some more commonly used characters that are not accessible directly from your keyboard have special shortcuts for accessing them. For example if you press ALT + CONTROL + C while editing text, a copyright symbol is accessed. See the table at the end for a complete listing of character shortcuts.

Special Functions

Shift Key

The SHIFT key in conjunction with other operations is used extensively in PagePlus.

Moving: If the SHIFT key is pressed when you are moving an object in PagePlus, the movement will be constrained to the direction of the next movement (either left/right or up/down). Releasing and then pressing the SHIFT key again will allow the constrain direction to be switched.

Sizing and creating: If the SHIFT key is pressed when you create or size an object, the size will be constrained. For boxes, the constraint will give a square; for ovals, a circle; for lines, a 45-degree line; and for pictures, the x–y ratio of the original picture is preserved.

Selecting objects: If the SHIFT key is pressed when you use the Pointer tool to select objects, the object you select will be added to/taken from the PagePlus group when you release the mouse button. You'll notice that if you hold the SHIFT key down, then press the mouse button down (but don't release), the object that will be added to/subtracted from the group will be highlighted.

Selecting region of text: If the SHIFT key is held down while cursoring within a text block, a region of text (shown in reverse) is selected.

Select All: If you have an object selected and you press the SHIFT key as you do the Edit/Select All operation, PagePlus will select all objects of the same types as the object selected rather than all the objects on the page.

ToolBox: If the SHIFT key is pressed at the time you select one of the creator (Box, Line, Oval) tools, the tool will not automatically switch back to the Pointer after the object is created. This is useful if you want to draw a sequence of lines, for example.

Using FTP to Transfer Files

Account information	account
ASCII: prepare to transfer an ASCII file	ascii
Binary: prepare to transfer a binary file	binary
Change directory	cd
Change directory on *your* system	lcd (use like the UNIX cd command)
Change directory to previous	cdup or cd ..
Close the connection	close or disconnect
Close the connection and exit FTP	bye or quit or Ctrl-d
Confirm transfer type	type
Connect to an FTP site	open *hostaddress* or ftp *hostaddress*
Current directory: show path	pwd
Directory listing: full	dir
Directory listing: names only	ls
Directory listing: names only, several columns	ls -x
Directory listing: include subdirectories and put in a text file	ls -lR *filename*
Exit FTP	quit or bye or press Ctrl-d
Hash marks indicate transfer progress	hash
Help: a list of FTP commands	help or ?
Help: describe a command	help *commandname* or ? *commandname*
Read a text file	get *filename* -
Read a text file using "more"	get *filename* - " l more"
Transfer a file from the FTP site	get *sourcefile destinationname*
Transfer a file to your computer with Xmodem	xmodem st *filename* (text file)
	xmodem sa *filename* (Apple text file)
	xmodem sb *filename* (binary file)
Transfer a file *from* your computer with Xmodem	xmodem rb *filename*
Transfer a file to your computer with Zmodem	sz *filename filename* *etc* (text file)
Transfer multiple files *from* the FTP site	mget *filename filename etc* or mget *partialname**
Transfer multiple files *to* the FTP site	mput *filename filename*
Uncompress UNIX compress files	uncompress *filename*

Using WAIS (the swais version)

Start WAIS	telnet to a WAIS site or run from service provider's menu
Deselect all selections	=
E-mail a document	m
Enter keywords on which to search	w and then press Enter. (Press Ctrl-C to cancel)
Move the cursor down one entry	j or down arrow or Ctrl-n
Move the cursor down one screen	J or Ctrl-v or Ctrl-d
Move the cursor up one entry	k or up arrow or Ctrl-p
Move the cursor up one screen	K or Ctrl-u
Move to a particular line	type the number and press Enter
Quit	q
Read about the highlighted database	v or , (comma)
Read a jumbled up document	Press l type more, and press Enter
Return to the listing	s
Search for a listing	Press / then type the word you are looking for and press Enter
Search selected entries with keywords	Enter
Select an entry	Spacebar
(or deselect a selected entry)	or . (period)
Select an entry and move to keywords field	Ctrl-j
View the Help screen	h or ?

Internet Survival Cheat Sheet

cut here

UNIX Commands

Backspace	**Backspace, Ctrl-h, #**
Cancel an operation	**Ctrl-C, q**
Change directory	**cd /***directoryname*
Change directory back one level	**cd ..** (leave a space after the d)
Change directory back to home directory	**cd**
Clear the command line	**Ctrl-U or @**
Copy a file	**cp** *oldname newname*
Copy a file to another directory	**cp** *oldname directoryname*
Copy several files to another directory	**cp** *firstpartofname* directoryname*
Current directory: show path	**pwd**
Delete a file	**rm** *filename*
List directory contents: full info and hidden files	**ls -al**
List directory contents: full information	**ls -l**
List directory contents: names only	**ls**
List directory contents: names only, several columns	**ls -x**
Logout	**Ctrl-d**, logout, exit
Move a file	**mv** *filename directoryname*
Password (change)	**passwd**
Read a text file	**cat** *filename*
Read a text file: page by page	**more** *filename*
Read the instruction manual	**man** *commandname* **??**
Rename a file	**mv** *originalname newname*
Repeat command	**!! or r**
Search for text in a file	**grep** *"this text" filename*

Telenet to Archie

Search type, selecting	**set search** *type* (*type* may be **regex, exact, sub,** or **subcase**)
Search type, finding	**show search**
Searching	**prog** *filename*
Paging, turn on	**set pager**
Paging, turn off	**unset pager**
E-mail a list	**mail** *emailaddress*
E-mail, set e-mail address	**set mailto** *emailaddress*
Descriptive search	**whatis** *keyword*
View a list of FTP sites	**list**
View a list of Archie servers	**servers**
Maxhits, modify the number	**maxhits** *number*

Telnet Sessions

Connect to a Telnet site	**open** *hostaddress* or **telnet** *hostaddress*
Connect to an IBM mainframe	**tn3270** *hostaddress*
Close Telnet connection from Telnet site	**quit, exit, Ctrl-d,** or **done.** Or try **Ctrl-]** followed by **close**
Close Telnet connection from telnet> prompt	**close**
Close a Telnet session	**quit, q,** or **Ctrl-d**
Select an escape character	**set escape** *character*
Turn echo on and off	**set echo**
Suspend the session	**z**
Restart session	**fg** (in most cases)
View help	**?**

alpha books

Control Key

Quick Copy: If you move an object while the CONTROL key is pressed, PagePlus will make and move a copy of the object, leaving the original unchanged.

Sizing and creating: When you paste or resize a picture, if the CONTROL key is pressed the picture size will be constrained to be a multiple of its original size, or in the case of bitmap-type pictures, the size will be constrained to sizes which produce good results on your currently selected printer in Windows.

Editing single text blocks: If you have the text tool selected and you double-click over a frame text block, while the CONTROL key is held down, the single text block, rather than the story to which it belongs, is loaded into WritePlus.

Escape Key

Pressing the ESCAPE key while in the middle of a sizing, moving, or creation operation will abort the operation. Pressing the ESCAPE key will allow the import of a text file to be aborted.

Function Keys

F1: This is a shortcut for accessing the PagePlus help. This is available at any time when the normal Help menu is available and is the equivalent of HELP/INDEX.

F2: When moving or dropping text into a frame that already contains text, the F2 key will switch between the text block dropping before or after the highlighted block.

F3: This causes PagePlus to delay most screen update operations until the key is released. For example, if you are editing a wrap outline while pressing the F3 key, any text will not reflow until after you release the key.

F4: If you are moving a block of frame text, pressing F4 will make it become free text. Similarly, when moving free text over a frame, pressing F4 will make that text become a block within that frame.

F5: This swaps between the tool currently selected on the ToolBox and the tool that was previously selected.

Character Shortcuts

PagePlus allows you to access certain characters using the following shortcuts. Remember that you can also use Edit/Character Map or use the Windows standard of pressing ALT + 0XXX where XXX is the reference number of the character you require—see your *Microsoft Windows User's Guide* for more details. Remember, if you require a symbol from a special font such as WingDings, you must select that font for your text as well as keying the character.

CONTROL + ALT + B	•	Bullet
CONTROL + /	†	Dagger
CONTROL + ALT + /	‡	Double dagger
CONTROL + ALT + =	—	Em-rule or dash
CONTROL + ALT + C	©	Copyright symbol
CONTROL + ALT + R	®	Registered symbol
CONTROL + ALT + T	™	Trademark symbol
CONTROL + [	'	Single open quote
CONTROL +]	'	Single close quote
CONTROL + ALT + [	"	Double open quote
CONTROL + ALT +]	"	Double close quote
CONTROL + ALT + ,	' '	Comma space
CONTROL + ALT + 1	' '	Digit space

CONTROL + ALT + N	' '	En-space
CONTROL + ALT + M	' '	Em-space
CONTROL + ALT + 2	"	Inch mark
CONTROL + ALT + '	'	Foot mark

Index